Pier Paolo Pasolini was born in Bologna in 1922 and died in mysterious circumstances at Rome in 1975. He was novelist, poet, critic, essayist and polemicist, as well as film director, and this journey to India was only one of his many travels. Yet meeting with people and customs so different from the Rome of his novels *Ragazzi di vita* and *Una vita violenta* or those of his adolescence *Atti Impuri* and *Amado Mio* left an indelible mark on his imagination, one determined by a love for 'primitive' places of the kind where *Oedipus Rex* and *Medea* were filmed. The markets of Calcutta, the processions on the Ganges and the craftsmen of Bombay evoked in his mind the eternal characters of fable, of epic stories, those who populated his filmed 'trilogy of life': *Decameron, the Canterbury Tales* and *A Thousand and One Nights*. In fact, to shoot this last film, Pasolini returned to the Indian peninsula, reconstructing in his 'search for lost peoples' that fragile connection existing between memories of a legendary past and the savage realities of the surrounding world. Among his other films should be mentioned *Accattone, Mamma Roma, The Gospel according to St. Matthew, Teorema, Porcile* and *Salò or the 100 days of Sodom.* His was one of the most attentive and profound voices of our time, as this work confirms.

The Scent of India

Pier Paolo Pasolini

Translated by David Price

Olive Press

First published in Great Britain in 1984 by
The Olive Press, 30 Pembroke Road, London, E17
Originally published as *L'Odore dell' India*
by Longanesi & C. S.p.A. (Milan) 1974

Second impression 1985

Translation © 1984 The Olive Press
Text and cover design by David Williams
Cover photo by Ian S. Robertson
Phototypeset by AKM Associates (UK) Ltd.,
Ajmal House, Hayes Road, Southall, London
Printed in Great Britain by Photobooks (Bristol) Limited

ISBN 0-946889-02-3

Trade distribution in Scotland, North of England,
Midlands, North Wales and Ireland by
Scottish and Northern Book Distribution,
4th floor, 18 Granby Row, Manchester 1 (061-228 3903)
and 48a, Hamilton Place, Edinburgh 3 (031-225 4950)

Trade distribution in South and
South West of England and South Wales by
GMP Publishers Limited, PO Box 247,
London N15 (01-800 5861)

Translator's note

Pasolini was perhaps above all a poet, and his prose often reflects this side of his character. In contrast to the polemical and discursive tone of his more iconoclastic essays, I have attempted to preserve the tenderness, the compression, and also the angular nature of his prose in this book. He chooses his words carefully and they are intended to resonate, to work hard. The result is close to poetry. Only when the sense becomes completely obscured in English, when his favoured passive voice or poetic repetitions sound merely stilted, have I changed the order or smoothed the texture of a sentence. Above all I have tried to retain the sound of an Italian writing about India, an Italian poet, while still presenting readable English, and in this I take the side of Nabokov rather than Edmund Wilson in that eternal debate on the 'correct' way to translate.

The Scent of India

I

Painful state of excitement on arrival. The Gateway to India. A section, phantasmagoric in nature, of Bombay. An enormous crowd dressed in towels. Moravia goes to bed: my exhibition of the intrepid spirit in venturing into the Indian night. The gentility of Sardar and of Sundar.

It is almost midnight. At the Taj Mahal the atmosphere is one of a market closing. The big hotel, one of the most famous in the world, is riddled from one side to the other by corridors and high saloons (like seeing the inside of an enormous musical instrument), peopled only by 'boys' clothed in white, and by porters in festive turbans waiting for dubious taxis to pass. It is not the moment, it is really not the moment to go to bed, in those rooms as big as dormitories, full of furniture of the miserable, retarded twentieth century, with ventilators which seem like helicopters.

These are the first hours of my presence in India, and I don't know how to calm the thirsty beast trapped within me as in a cage. I persuade Moravia to make at least a short stroll outside the hotel, and to breathe a little of the air of our first Indian night.

So we go out through the secondary exit on to the narrow sea promenade that runs behind the hotel. The sea is calm, giving no sign of its presence. Along the little embankment which contains it there are some cars parked and, near to them, are those fabulous beings without roots, without consciousness, full of ambiguous and disturbing meaning, but endowed with powerful fascination, who are the first Indians with experiences, experiences which desire to be exclusive, like mine.

They are all beggars, or the kind of people who live

at the edges of a big hotel, experts in its functional and secret life: they wear a white rag which covers their thighs, another rag on their shoulders and, some of them, another rag around the head: they are almost all black-skinned, like negroes, some very black.

There is a group of them under the porticoes of the Taj Mahal, towards the sea, youngsters and boys: one of them is mutilated, with 'corroded' limbs, and is stretched out wrapped in his rags as if he were in front of a church instead of a hotel. The others wait, silent, ready.

I don't yet understand what their duty or their hope is. I look at them sideways on, chattering with Moravia, who was here 24 years ago and knows the world well enough not to be in the painful state I find myself.

On the sea there is no light, no sound: here we are almost at the point of a long peninsula, a horn of the bay which forms the port of Bombay: the port is in the distance. Under the little wall there are only some ships, bare and empty. At a few metres distance, against the sea and the summer heavens, rises up the Gateway of India.

It is a kind of triumphal arch, with four gothic portals, of a quite severe *liberty* style: its mass imposes itself on the edge of the Indian Ocean as if visibly joining it with the interior land, which, at that point, forms a round square with some gloomy gardens and constructions, all large, floral and a little dissipated like the Taj Mahal itself. It is earthy and artificial in colour, standing amidst the scattered immobile lamps in the peace of deep summer.

Again at the edges of this large symbolic gateway, there are other figures from the European prints of the 17th century: little Indians, their thighs enveloped in a

11

white drape and, above faces as dead as the night, the circle of a narrow turban of rags. Only that, when seen close up, these rags are lurid with a miserable, natural dirt, very prosaic in comparison to the figurative suggestions of an epoch at which they, in every other sense, have come to a halt. They are still young beggars, or survivors, tarrying by night in the places which by day are probably the centre of their activities. They look askance at us, I and Moravia, letting us go: their inexpressive eye cannot see in us anything promising. On the contrary, they almost close in on themselves as we walk tiredly along the little chestnut-coloured parapet.

□   □   □

And so like this we arrive under the Gateway of India which from close-by is bigger than it seems from a distance. The doors at an acute angle, and the walls triforated, of a yellowish and pallid colour, loom over our heads with the solemnity of certain entrance halls of Northern stations. But within, in the shadow of the arch, a song can be heard: there are two, three voices which are singing together, strongly, continuously, with fervor.

The tone, the significance and the simplicity are those of any youngsters' song that one can hear in Italy or Europe: but these are Indians, the melody is Indian. It is like the first time anyone sings in the world. At least for me: I feel the life of another continent like another world, without relation to anything I know, a world which is almost autonomous, with other inner laws of its own: virgin.

It seems to me that to hear that song of Bombay youngsters under the Gateway of India takes on an

12

ineffable and extra meaning: a revelation, a life's conversion. I can do nothing but let them sing, trying to spy on them from the imitation marble corner of the great Gothic gateway: they are stretched out on the bare pavement, under the dark mantle of the pointed arch, in the filtered milky light that comes from the square onto the sea. Clothed with white rags round their hips and with those dark heads: one cannot make out their age. Their song is completely without joy. It follows a single musical phrase, breathless and grieving.

All is precipitated in this moment of heavy, murky peace. Our arrival in Bombay from the sky: slimy mountain sides, reddish, corpse-like, between little green marshes and an endless landslide of slums, depots, miserable new suburbs that looked like the innards of a split carcass, hundreds of thousands of little precious stones, green, yellow, white, which were gently shining: the first porters met under the belly of the aeroplane, black like demons clothed in red tunics: the first Indian faces when scarcely out of the airport, the taxi-drivers, their helpers the boys, dressed like ancient Greeks: and the road like a cleft towards the city.

An hour's drive along an unconfined periphery made up completely of little huts, clumps of shops, shadows of the banjan tree on the little Indian houses with their rounded corners all triforated like old furniture, leaking light, cross-roads thronged with shoeless people dressed like in the Bible, red and yellow double-decker trams. Modern apartment buildings immediately aged by the tropical humidity, standing amidst muddy gardens and tenement houses of wood, bluish, green, or simply corroded by the humidity and the sun: infinite layers to the crowd, with a sea of

13

lights as if everywhere in that city of six million inhabitants there was a street carnival. Then the centre, sinister and new, Malabar Hill with its residential blocks worthy of Parioli[1] amidst the old bungalows, and the endless promenade a series of light globes which were filtering into the water as far as the eye could see . . .

The cows on the streets, which were moving with the crowd, squatting with the squatters, walking about with those just walking about, stopping with those stopping: poor cows with their coats turned into mud, obscenely skinny, some as little as dogs, consumed by fasting, with eyes eternally attracted by objects and destined for eternal disillusion. It was almost nightfall and they were squatting at the cross-roads under some traffic light or another, in front of the main doors of disordered public buildings: black heaps, grey with hunger and bewilderment.

□   □   □

Revolving around them, life had the same relaxed rhythm as those poor animals. You only needed to see the patience with which the people waited at the bus-stop for the bus. They made a queue which the Swiss or the Germans would not dream of: without shouldering one another, one at a time, concentrating. Some were dressed, more or less, in the European style, with white trousers, broad at the ankles, clumsily put on, and a large white shirt: others, and there were more of them, were dressed with a kind of sheet between the legs, full of large knots at the stomach, while their calves, black, forming a bow, were left completely bare: and above this sheet was either a shirt or a European jacket, and on the head was bound the usual rag.

Others were dressed in wide white trousers of Arabic form, with a white tunic above, transparent: others again wore a pair of shorts, very wide, from which their dry black legs descended like the clappers of a bell and above, almost completely covering the trousers, was a fluttering shirt. The women were all in saris, braceleted: and the sari was of various colours, from simple ones made of rags to those liturgical ones of drapes, woven with ancient and refined craftsmanship.

This enormous crowd practically dressed in towels breathed a sense of misery, of unspeakable poverty. It seemed as if they had all just escaped from an earthquake and, happy to have survived, had made themselves content with the few rags with which they had fled from their pitiful destroyed beds, from the most appalling slums.

Just look at them there, two of the fugitives who are singing together under the Gateway of India, waiting for the arrival of sleep in the warm summer night.

Held within their life, of which I have on my retina only a first sketch of the outer surface, they are singing a song (as old and familiar to them as it is pure novelty to me) and I demand of it that it express something inexpressible, something which only the days ahead waiting for me here, from tomorrow onwards, will be able to gently exorcise and put into perspective.

However at this point Moravia decides that it *is* time to be tired and, with his admirable fastidiousness, halts and turns decisively towards the Taj Mahal. But I don't. Since I am not exhausted (uneconomic as I am) I do not give up.

I decide to wander round alone a little more. I go towards those gloomy gardens under the expansive buildings, which stand a the bottom of the square by the sea. On the right there is a dark palace which seems made of terracotta, in twentieth century style with allusions to Indian taste; on the left another hotel with a portico in front; and a petrol station; and an esplanade with traffic lights, and then farther on, after a bend, an immense oval square all surrounded by palms, ashen in the filtered, impure light of the moon. A landscape in the style of an exotic postcard of the nineteenth century, like a tapestry of Porta Portese.[2] In the immense oval clearing someone is still moving, dressed in his white rags.

Some youngsters are silently playing with a few clubs: others are crouched down with their knees at the height of their face, their arms dangling balanced on their knees. An occasional taxi still passes: the night is warm and empty, like in holiday resorts at the height of summer.

I turn back towards the hotel. In front of a building, now without any lights, which is both cinema and meeting place, (the Regal), a boy approaches me with his wide shorts like skirts, wearing a dirty shirt above. He lets me know that he is disposed to offer me something: in the first place to get me some alcohol, because there is prohibition in Bombay: and then of course anything else. He believes me to be a sailor disembarked from some ship. I give him a rupee and leave him: I am intimidated, not understanding anything about him.

There are others similar to him in the neighbourhood: on the pavements, which are warm and full of dry old dust, and under the cadaverous buildings. They look at me and say nothing. They mind their own business.

□   □   □

In front of the hotel with the porticoes a whole group of them is bunched on the ground in the dust: limbs, rags and shadows get mixed together. Seeing me pass, two or three get up and follow behind me, as if waiting. Then I stop and smile at them, uncertain.

A black one, thin, with a delicate Aryan face and an enormous pile of black hair, greets me, then approaches me barefoot, his rags around him, one between his legs, one on his shoulders; behind him appears another, glossy black this one, with a big negroid mouth on which the down of adolescence is shadowed. Yet when he smiles, there flames behind his black face an immaculate candour: a flash within, a wind, a blaze that removes the black layer from the white layer which is his inner smile.

The first one is called Sundar, the second one Sardar. One is Muslim, the other Hindu. Sundar comes from Hyderabad, where he has his family: he is seeking his fortune in Bombay like a Calabrian boy might come to Rome: in a city where he knows no one, doesn't have a house, must arrange a bed just as it happens, and eat when he can. He coughs, from a small bird-like thorax: – perhaps he is consumptive. The Muslim religion gives to his sweet, delicate face a certain air of timid shrewdness, whereas the other one, Sardar, is all sweetness and devotion: Hindu to the bone.

He comes from far Andhra, the region of Madras: he also is without a family, without a house, without anything.

The others, their friends, have remained behind in the shadow of the hotel's secondary door. But now I see them move, in silence. They hunch around a large paper bag which they open on the dusty pavement.

17

I ask Sardar and Sundar what they are doing. They
are eating the *pudding*, the left-overs of hotel suppers.
They eat in silence like dogs, but without fighting,
with the reasonableness, and sweetness of the Hindu.

Sardar and Sundar look at them along with me,
wearing a smile as if to say that they also act like that
and, if I hadn't been there, they also would be eating
those scraps at this very moment. Instead we go to
have a walk in the neighbourhood.

The streets are deserted by now, lost in their dusty,
dry, dirty silence. They have something about them
which is grandiose as well as miserable. This is the
central, modern part of the city, but with the corrosion
of the stones, the shutters, and the woodwork is like
an ancient village.

Almost all of the dilapidated houses have a little
portico in front of them: and here . . . I stand face to
face with one of the most impressive facts about India.

All the porticoes, *all* the pavements spill over with
sleepers. They are stretched out on the earth, against
the columns, against the walls, against the doorposts.
Their rags envelop them entirely, smeared with filth.
Their sleep is so deep that they seem like the dead,
wrapped in torn, fetid shrouds.

They are made up of youngsters, boys, old men, and
women with children. They sleep rolled up or
stretched out, in their hundreds. Some of them are still
awake, especially the boys: they pause to turn round
or to speak quietly, seated at the door of a closed shop,
or on the steps of a house. Someone stretches out at
that moment and turns round in his sheet, covering
his head. The whole street is full of their silence: and
their sleep is similar to death. Yet to a death which, in
its turn, is as gentle as sleep.

Sardar and Sundar look at them with the same smile

with which they were watching their friends devour the remains of the *pudding*: they also will sleep like this soon.

They accompany me towards the Taj Mahal . . . Just look at the Gateway of India against the sea. The song has ceased: the two boys that were singing must now be sleeping on the bare pavement, in their rags. Already I have learnt something from their song. A horrendous poverty.

Sardar and Sundar politely take their leave of me, a smile of solar brilliance within their gloomy faces. They don't expect me to give them some rupees: therefore they take them full of joyful surprise. Sardar grips my hand and kisses it, saying to me: "You are a good sir".

I leave them, touched in my heart like an idiot. Something has already begun.

II

No state religion! A fragment of the ancient Greek rites at Chopati. Other judicious observations of the Indian religious customs. Hands clasped at Aurangabad. A revelation: the way in which the Indian says yes.

At New Delhi I went with Moravia to a reception at
the Cuban Embassy, in honour of the second
anniversary of their revolution. In front of a small villa
in that immense garden-city, which – just as I imagine
it must be at Washington – is in fact Delhi, a huge red
and blue tent had been erected, with a pavement of red
carpets. There the whole diplomatic corps of the
capital thronged together, from the ambassador of
Yugoslavia to that of Belgium, the cultural attaché of
Cuba to that of Russia: all with their glass of whisky
in their hand, all lined up as on a print, indulging in a
pleasant babble of conversation amidst the rather cold
spring air.

In the middle of the elegant shapes of diplomats and
their wives an absurd image appeared to me (it was
only ten days since I had left Italy, but it seemed to me
like ten years): two Catholic priests, thin as spades,
with their hips held by a red belt and a red cape on the
back of their neck. They must have been Spanish: they
had the air of swordsmen.

For me they were emblems, cogent emblems of a
whole world.

But for how many millions of people in the Indian
world were they nothing but a vivacious flourish of
red and black, put there by a potentate so far away as
to seem non-existent?

It will seem absurd, but for the first time I had the
impression that Catholicism does not coincide with

reality: yet the separation of the two entities was so unexpected and violent that it constituted a kind of trauma . . . then I asked myself, for the first time with urgency, what this immense world might be filled with, this subcontinent of four hundred million souls. I had been in India for too short a period to find something which could supplant my being used to *state* religion: the religious freedom was a kind of blank space I faced with dizziness.

Only a little at a time would I get used to this condition of free religious choice, which on the one hand gives a sense of the needlessness of all religion, and on the other is so rich with pure religious spirit.

To draw a picture of Indian religion is impossible so I will limit myself to putting together some little fragments of the unrealisable mosaic.

I was going down from Malabar Hill to Bombay, with kilometres of road already under my boots, and was walking by the side of the sea. It was the hour of dusk. The lamps of the endless embankment had recently been lit.

I liked to walk alone, quiet, learning to get to know that new world step by step, just as I had got to know the outskirts of Rome by walking alone and silent. It was somewhat similar: only now everything seemed drawn-out and vague on an unclear background.

In the centre of the big semi-circle between the seafront and the water stretched an expanse of sand, which was dark with the first shadows of the evening and vast like a market: Chopati was its name, and it was the place of big political meetings, one of Nehru's great arenas. Now it was seething with crowds of people taking the air, walking, contemplating the sea. There must have been two or three thousand people in that circle of sand: a space almost silent, beyond the confused line of traffic along the seafront, which was made up of little taxis and lop-sided buses. Some crouched with their knees at the height of their faces, their hands abandoned over their knees: some squatted in the Indian style with their legs laid one over the other in the shape of a cross: while others stood on their feet, their pitiful rags wrapped round them, which became ever more lustrous as the sun slowly sunk behind the milky horizon.

In the middle of this crowd sellers of tidbits, unpronounceable sweets (like the American nuts and ice-cream in our own country), were passing carrying a brilliant little white flame on their trays: the little flames crossing each other in the middle of the silent throng.

A wall of bigger flames was glowing in the background in a corner of the beach dedicated to the little floats of the sellers. An occasional child was still flying his little four-cornered eagle, blue and rust, against the blue and rust sky: by the side of a kind of canopy a blind lady was singing, while two little children wearing serious expressions were playing on the necks of deafening instruments, similar to castanets. At one point on the beach there was a large image of Vishnu, constructed with sand but adorned with stones and coloured materials; and here and there were circles of people standing to listen to a kind of sung story which told a serious tale with all the ingenious dramatic art of the Indian, a tale both simple and didactic.

I don't know how I managed in the middle of such a crowd, amidst the flames which crossed it from every side, to pick out a group of people who were there for a very special and exceptional reason. It was probably because of their preoccupied and secretive attitude, and their decisive gestures.

I counted thirteen people in all. Four women, of whom the eldest would have been about forty and the youngest almost an adolescent with a suckling baby at her breast: two men of about thirty, an old man and a young man: and some children. This whole group, which was clearly two or three related families, was walking quickly through the middle of the crowd at Chopati, and I, at first with great discretion and then ever more openly, followed them.

Two of the women, the eldest and obviously mothers, were carrying trays, one of bronze and one of wood, piled with fruit, bananas, coconuts, pineapples, and bunches of little flowers in vases. There must also have been some cooked vegetables and some rice.

The group stopped just at the edge of the sea. It was low tide, and in front of them extended a kind of marsh formed by grey mud, which was still full of little wells of water. As the sun went down, it gave the colour of silver to its patina: bronzed silver the mud, clear silver the water; an immense embroidery of silver.

The women put their trays down on the sand and the children began to play round about them, some of them running, some of them playing little games with their hands in the sand: without anybody shouting at them or calling them to order. Of the rest even the adults were carrying out their ritual with great humility and distance, without great preoccupation, without visible devotion.

One man took a fruit, a mango or a lemon, drew – so it seemed – a kind of circle on the heads of some of those present, especially the children, and approached the silvery edge of the crystal water in front of him, making a gesture of throwing it into the water; then,

24

as if reconsidering it, he proceeded further onto the silvery expanse, becoming a kind of magic shadow, whose gestures became indistinguishable. Then he turned back to the group of friends.

The women, on the other hand, guided by the old woman, were making a kind of strange procession around the trays, with all the measured, resigned gestures of women in the kitchen: they changed the places of the fruit, the little flowers, the little bowls of cooked rice: and lit some pieces of perfumed taper, which began to slowly burn. Then the men brought out some bags of leather sacking, and all set to work to fill these bags with the offerings. It was always the old woman who guided the operation. The men obeyed her, patiently and subordinately, putting the force and prestige they have as men into the rite, but without any notion of responsibility. That they left totally to the old woman, almost with a kind of pleasure in their temporary lack of responsibility, and in the hope that this rite, which was directed by the mother, would bear some fruit, perhaps some good, for the whole family.

(This situation was not new to me: even among the peasants of the Friuli something similar occurs, in certain rustic habits left over from pagan times: the men, even if it is ironic, act as if neutered and silenced: their force and modernity grow quiet before the capricious mystery of the gods of tradition.)

When the bags which were in the hands of the men were full, the women stayed near the empty trays, with the still burning tapers and with the children who were quietly playing: and the men, who had heard the final command, ventured to complete the last part of the ritual alone, going far off on the network of silver as tenuous and dazzling as the stained glass of a cathedral which swallowed up their shadows.

In the meantime as I was watching an old man had come to my side. He had long black hair held up by a fetid turban and a large black beard: he was wrapped around in white rags, and looked me up and down with a kind of smirk.

I looked at him closer: he was no bigger than a sickly and ill-formed adolescent: dry, fragile, like a featherless animal: his movements had the delicacy and the restrained hysteria of those of a little child.

I understood that his was a smile of complicity. I also understood that he was standing there waiting for the family to go away in order to eat their offerings. And finally I understood that he was half dead of hunger. That ashamed smile was simply meant to say: "Now I am going to grab that food and to eat it for myself like a dog. You understand me, don't you? Well it's ridiculous, but it's just one of those things which happen to anyone, if they are hungry enough, is that not true?"

So the long wait for those two who had gone beyond the silver water-line to reach the sea, in the feverish shadows of the dark, gradually became a torment.

Finally the two reappeared against the immaculate silver stripe; then the hungry old man ran towards the sea like a baby girl and disappeared into the shadow from which the two young fathers were emerging: satisfied, silent, welcomed by the tumblings of their children and by the tranquil silence of the women. And the family prepared to return towards their house, across the beach that appeared to be crowded by an army of souls.

It was not always the case that I saw this peace, both humble and human, in the Indian rites. In fact, on the contrary I often saw some shocking things. A tour of a

26

whole series of splendid temples in the South, from
Madras to Thanjavur, a dozen stupendous visits, was
disturbed by watching the crowd round the temples
and their messy devotions.

At Calcutta, a terrifying vision. It was impossible to
go to see the temple of Kali, which is one of the few
curiosities of that sinister and hopeless place, and one
of the world's largest human conglomerations.

We arrived, descended from the taxi and were
assailed, as if by a swarm of mosquitoes, by a vast
crowd of lepers, of blind people, of mutilated people, of
beggars. Then we turned towards the little central
court of the temple (without managing to see it, such
was the terrible crowd which was tormenting us: in
any case it was a modern construction, without any
stylistic value). Having arrived in the courtyard,
between a whirlwind of rags and poor naked limbs, we
saw someone leading a little goat towards a kind of
scaffold, a split piece of wood placed on the pavement.
A curved blade rose in the air, the head of the goat
rolled to earth, and the circle of its neck filled with a
boiling foam of blood.

Life in India has the characteristic of being
insupportable: who knows how they survive eating
spoons of dirty rice, drinking filthy water, under the
continuous threat of cholera, of typhus, of smallpox,
even of the plague, sleeping on the earth or in
atrocious dwellings. Every morning awakening must
be a nightmare. And yet the Indians get up with the
sun, resigned, and resigned they begin to give
themselves something to do: it is a matter of vacantly
wandering the whole day, a little bit as one sees at
Naples, but here with incomparably more miserable
results. It is true that the Indians are never happy:
they often smile, that's true, but they are smiles of

sweet resignation, not of happiness.

And yet every now and then someone spills out of this terrifying vortex, this infernal tempest. He is seen deposited on the edge, stunned. It often happened that I met someone with their eyes staring into vacancy, unmoving: the clear symptoms of neurosis in their face. It seemed as if they had understood the insupportability of this existence. Those expressions of abstraction from life, of renunciation, of arrest or iciness.

I saw them all concentrated on the face of a young man at Aurungabad. Aurungabad is a little town two hundred miles from Bombay, the usual informal mass of houses clumsily leaning one against the other, filthy quarters and bazaars stretching out along an irregular central street, beyond the open tunnels of the drains.

In the centre of this street there was a tree, immense and stupendous, as the trees often are in India, and around this tree a little cage painted in red and other lively colours. Opposite the cage, as I was passing by in my frantic researches, I saw a young man, immobile, pale, abstract: but in his absent eyes there was great order and great peace. He held his hands together. I approached to see better. He was shoeless, his shoes were there beside him on the putrid dusty earth. He was standing erect, immobile, like iron: made up of pure silence. I looked at what he was adoring. It was a frog, as high as a metre, enclosed within a little temple, and beyond it some dirty yellow carpets: a frog of wet wood, painted with red on its back and yellow on its stomach. In reality it was a degenerate form of the sacred cow: a true horror. I looked at the face of the young man who was praying: it was sublime.

I do not really know what Indian religion may be.

Read the articles of my admirable travelling companion Moravia, who has read up on the matter to perfection and, endowed with a greater capacity for synthesis than me, has very clear, well-based ideas on the theme. I know that in substance Brahminism speaks of an original vital force, a blast of "wind" that then manifests itself and becomes concrete in the infinite plasticity of things. In other words it is a little bit like the theory of atomic science. Indeed, just as Moravia reveals.

I have tried to speak of this with many Hindu: but nobody has even the faintest idea about it. Each one has his own cult, Vishnu, Siva or Kali, and he faithfully follows its rites. Of these I can only limit myself to some descriptions like those I have made. However one thing I can say: that the Hindu are the kindest, sweetest, gentlest people it is possible to know. Non-violence is in their roots, the reason itself of their life. Perhaps sometimes it defends its weakness with a little histrionicism or insincerity: but they are little shadows at the edges of so much light, of so much transparency.

It is sufficient to see how they say *yes*. Instead of agreeing like us by raising and lowering their head, they turn it around like when we say *no*: however the difference of the gesture is enormous. Their *no* which signifies *yes* consists in making the head undulate (their brown, wavy head with poor dark skin, which is yet the most beautiful colour which a skin can have) tenderly. It is a gesture which is at once sweet: – "Poor me, I say yes without knowing whether it can be done", and embarrassed: "Why not?", timid: "It is so difficult", and indulgent: "I am all for you". The head goes up and down as if gently detached from the neck and the shoulders rise a little with the gesture of

29

a young girl conquering her shame, who yet shows herself to be affectionate. Seen from a distance the Indian masses fix themselves in the memory with that gesture of agreement, and the childish and radiant smile in their eyes which accompanies it. Their religion is in that gesture.

III

The story of Revi

We are in Benares and we are walking, we veterans of the bazaar, guided by a Mohammedan taxi-driver as big, intelligent and fast as a European, towards the taxi. We are walking through a wide street in the centre, with houses on two storeys, puffed up like pianolas, completely made of wood, with circular rounded corners, the porticoes jagged and yet painted in soft colours.

From under a portico, freshly painted in bright green, amidst the confusion of taxis, drapes and cows, we hear the insistent, primitive sound of music. The face of the taxi-driver tells us this is something good: and so we approach and join a little throng grouped around a small window, in a street perpendicular to the main street and the green loggia. Through the window we see a small room, not very large at all and completely bare of ornament, if not plain dirty: some Hindus are crouched in line along the floor, six or seven lines with about ten people in each. All are singing with great fervour. The musical instruments that are accompanying this choir are few. There predominates a taut drum hit with great energy by the musician, who makes his hands appear as if detached in a whirlwind from the skin of the drum, as if the skin were smeared with oil. The blows are ordered but precipitous as well as dramatic. The song of the crouching crowd, although elementary – like the Indian melody – has something merry about it: it reminds us of songs in our own bars.

Under the window in a corner of the room there is a parapet painted yellow, which surrounds the chapel with the usual god symbol the *ingam*, whatever its sex, amongst the other figures in symbolic attention: an art both from folklore and modern.

Appearing from who knows where, someone mysterious begins to dance in front of the rail of the small altar, on the faded and torn carpet. He is a male jester, very adult and hairy, but clothed as a female fool: a large yellow cotton shirt and green body; bracelets at the wrists and at the ankles: necklaces and glittering earings. Between his fingers he rattles some bells, which merge with the sound of the other instruments, rattles them obsessively. To the deafening rhythm of his bells the jester dances in a circle, always making the same gestures: he turns on an axis of himself, making his skirt a kind of wheel. He stops, he turns again. He goes towards the crowd, makes the gesture of taking something on the palm of his open and outstretched hand, and then goes to throw this something towards the altar. He repeats these gestures without pausing, with the timbrel which snarl and snarl like a den of furious apes.

The expression of the fool has something obscene about it, something malignant. Among all those sweet Indian faces he is the only one to know what ugliness is. He knows it in a way which is both infantile and bestial, and he completes his sacred and antique dance as if making a caricature of it, denigrating it with his strange, treacherous vulgarity.

This wasn't the only case. Also at Gwalior, a little town between Delhi and Benares, I noted something similar. We were passing through the central part of the city, astonished by its modern aspect; a large Post

Office between three red and white apartment buildings, a big garden in the centre. However, everywhere in the middle of the traffic were cows and goats, grey with filth. Amidst the cows and goats, on a pavement was stretched out a sack, also grey with dirt, and beneath it a man, with a large black head of hair which extended from the edges of the sack. A group of people were standing around him or were on their knees venerating him. Before going away someone that had been there in devoted attention kissed him and then stroked his feet with his hand. And he, the adored one, was rigid under the filthy sheet, with all those dirty locks of hair stretched out on the pavement. When someone, paralysed with veneration approached him offering him a lighted cigarette, the adored one refused it, silently, limiting himself to scratching a foot obsessively, as if giving little nervous hysterical kicks to the entire world.

The day after at Khajuraho we had occasion to see another of these saints. Khajuraho is the most beautiful place in India, in fact perhaps the only place one could really say is beautiful in the *western* sense of that word. An immense garden meadow in the English style, green, of overwhelming softness, with some bouganvillea scattered near the large circular rocks, where the eye can lose itself in the enjoyment of a paradisical redness for hours on end. Lines of young girls with their saris, all of them wearing rings, were working on the meadow: and beyond, lines of boys squatting on the grass, and even beyond that youngsters who were carrying buckets of water at the end of poles: all in the peace of an eternal Spring. And scattered on these meadows were little temples: they are amongst the most sublime one can see in India.

At the edge of the meadow there was a little house,

a hut in good condition, made of stones: a lit fire within, and some furniture. Someone was hurrying about as if obsessed by his duties. He was a man of forty, with a cultivated black beard and a black moustache in the style of D'Artagnan. His looks immediately repelled me. Observing him well one saw that in fact he wasn't doing anything, wasn't occupied in lighting the fire, cooking beans or whatever. Yet with the same attention, accuracy and devotion of someone doing a job which is considered indispensable, he was taking part in a sacred ceremony. He was moving around the hut like a madman, stopping, touching objects, making gestures with his hands, bending towards the earth.

We left him there locked in his maniacal concentration, his endless circle of tolerance.

We couldn't manage to drag ourselves away from Khajuraho: there were six temples, small but stupendous, and we toured around each one for at least an hour, sat on its steps or on the meadow below, enjoying that unexpected peace, so powerful and so silent.

The temples in front of us, with their two parts (one the large part with the *ingam* inside, the other opposite and smaller, little more than a roof to cover the stupendous cow of stone facing the *ingam*) laid out in the gold light of the sun, were of an inexhaustible beauty. They didn't seem like things of stone: but of a material which was almost inflammable, more than just precious, ethereal. Large and small clouds descended onto that luscious green meadow, condensed, coagulated, became similar to large clusters of grapes with their feet fixed in the earth like dew drops, and it seemed as if the huge roofs were mated one on the other: and then, a little at a time, the patient sun appeared to have dried them out to the extent of rendering them like sugar, cane, wood, tufa: but leaving on every surface that network of woven grain, curled in the sun.

We were watching, seated on a jagged step made of a material which was both softness and age, with the world of temples around us, when we were distracted by a figure who was crossing the meadow. He was coming forward confidently, quickly: the gardeners round about bald and lazy, were deferentially watching him pass.

He was *the saint*. Who knows where he was going? He was walking impetuously, as naked as a worm, with a large moustache and a big black beard which went up and down with the movement of his elastic, almost athletic step: he walked tall with his chest puffed out, not even deigning to give a look to the faithful. He seemed like the head of an office who passes through the corridor between ushers and porters. And when a small poor black person very humbly went up to him and offered him the usual lighted cigarette, he didn't even turn, neither to thank him nor to even look at him, that imbecile.

Fortunately Hinduism is not a state religion. For that reason the *saints* are not dangerous. While their faithful admire them (too much really) there is always a Muslim, a Buddhist or a Catholic who looks at them with compassion, irony and curiosity. It is a fact however that in India the atmosphere is favourable to religiosity, as even the most simple reports tell us. Yet as far as I am concerned this doesn't mean that the Indians are very occupied by serious religious problems. Certain of their forms of religion *are* coercive, typically mediaeval: alienations due to the horrendous economic and hygienic situation of the country, real mystical neuroses, which remind one of the European ones, indeed of the Middle Ages, and these can afflict individuals or entire communities. But more than a specific religiosity (of the type which produces mystical phenomena or clerical power) I have observed amongst the Indians a generic and diffuse religiosity: a by-product of religion. The non-violence, in other words, the gentleness, the goodness of the Hindu. They have perhaps lost contact with the direct sources of their religion (which is evidently a degenerate religion) but they continue to be the living fruits of it. So their religion, which is the most abstract and philosophic in the world in theory, is now in reality a totally practical religion: a way of living.

One reaches thereby a kind of paradox: the Indians, abstract and philosophical by origin, are actually a practical people (be it simply a practicality which serves for living in an absurd human situation), while the Chinese, practical and empirical by origin, are actually an extremely ideological and dogmatic people (be it by solving a situation practically which appeared insoluble).

So in India now, more than just for the maintenance of religion, the atmosphere is propitious for some kind of practical religious spirit.

I have known some religious Catholics: and I must say that never has the spirit of Christ seemed to me so vivid and gentle: a transplant splendidly achieved. At Calcutta, Moravia, Morante and I went to meet Sister Teresa, a sister who is dedicated to the lepers. There are sixty thousand lepers at Calcutta, and some millions in the whole of India. It is one of the many terrible aspects of this nation, in the face of which one is completely powerless: at certain moments I felt some real attacks of hatred against Nehru and his hundred intellectual collaborators educated at

Cambridge: but I must say that I was unjust, because truly one must recognise that there is very little to be done in that situation. Sister Teresa tries to do something: as she says, only initiatives of her sort can help, because they begin from nothing. Leprosy, seen from Calcutta, has an horizon of sixty thousand lepers. Seen from Delhi the horizon is infinite.

Sister Teresa lives in a house not far from the centre of the city, in a dilapidated street worn down by the monsoons and by a misery which takes away your breath. With her there are another five or six sisters who help her to direct the organisation of research and the cure of lepers, and above all of assistance at their death: they have a little hospital where the lepers are taken to die.

Sister Teresa is an old woman, brown of skin, because she is Albanian, tall, dry, with two almost masculine cheek-bones, and a gentle eye which "sees" wherever it looks. In an impressive way she resembles a famous Saint Anna of Michelangelo: and on her features is impressed true goodness, of the type described by Proust in his old maid Françoise: goodness without sentimental additions, without expectations, both tranquil and tranquillising, powerful and practical.

On the other hand Father Wilbert is quite different! Perhaps because he is younger ... But the way that I came to know him was much less simple than making an ordinary visit: it constituted a true happening ...

The matter went briefly like this.

◻   ◻   ◻

We were two days from Cochin, a city of the Kerala, in the South of India. The Kerala is the poorest region of

India, but at the same time the most beautiful and the most modern. For some years the government has been Communist and the Communists are still very strong. The ports of the Kerala had the most ancient contacts with Europe. The first Christians, converted by St. Thomas it is said, are as old as the Europeans: the Arabs, the Portugese, the Dutch behaved here just as at home (massacring, exploiting, converting). Indeed at Cochin, which is a stupendous port, at the entry of which – between pacific lagoons – stretch out islands which seem to be the Terrestrial Paradise, one doesn't have very much of an impression of being in India: the great Indian softness is a little less obvious, and so too is the filth. The way of saying *yes* does not have that wonderful undulating of the head of a girl at her first communion, which is a regular gesture in the whole of India. There is a large percentage of old and new Catholics, many Muslims: and the Hindus are a little weakened through long contact with them. Every day, two or three boats arrive and sailors from every nation disembark. Here is all the toughness and corruption of a great international port. In this quite modern atmosphere the terrifying aspects of India are rendered even more terrifying. Here there are rickshaws carried by hand: I had to take one at Cochin in the middle of the night to return to the hotel, the *Malabar*, which is situated on an island in the middle of the port, in a wasteland of docks and deposits the length of eight miles. However I didn't have the courage to let myself be carried: so I went the whole eight miles on foot, chattering with Josef the rickshaw man, amidst the fearsome night of this deserted port. Josef had been a sailor and had travelled the whole world. He knew Genova and Naples, but the city he preferred was New York. Now he was ill: certainly consumptive. He had seven, eight children to maintain, and so he had been reduced to horse work, running between those two repulsive pieces of wood on his cart.

We had been two days at Cochin: it was Sunday. I had wanted to stay alone, because only alone, abandoned, silent, on foot, do I manage to get in contact with things. For that reason I left Moravia and Elsa Morante, who went to make a tour with the Ford driven by the gentle Tayaram through the city: and I set out from the hotel on foot.

Immediately the usual parade of rags, of sick people, of ruffians, appeared around me like a swarm of mosquitoes. I chose Josef at once, old Josef, shaven, in his Sunday shirt, standing by his lugubrious rickshaw.

I made a pretence of getting on, and as soon as we were a little distant, in the middle of a parade of shops, I got off and said to Josef that I would prefer to make a trip by boat, on the lagoons in front of the port.

But just then Revi detached himself from the swarm of ragged people, of sick and ruffians, and, in the distance, was now following us: just over there, clothed in white, with the long cotton shirt tails which flutter around the ankles and the little tunic around the body which caressed his hips in a thousand folds, hips which from close up were dirty, but from a distance were of the most pure whiteness.

I had got to know him when I arrived at Cochin: it was the hour of dusk and, with Moravia and Elsa, we had gone out to make a little tour from the *Malabar Hotel*, along the port: deserted, alone with some porter, a white figure against the entangled outline of red and black ships. Revi was there with his little companion on a stretch of dirty sand between two dark shops and a few decrepit enclosures. They called me out of the blue to start up a conversation: they asked me if I was

40

a sailor, where I was from, how long I was staying at Cochin. Then two ruffians approached wrapped in their sheets. They were also hospitable but with something sinister in their look. Finally a banana was produced from I don't know where which was offered to me for sale: I bought it, gave the money to Revi, but as he went away I chanced to see the others take it from his hand.

From then on I always glimpsed Revi near to the hotel, with his happy little face and his billowing rags. That evening too when I returned late on foot with Josef and the rickshaw, he appeared in the middle of the endless, extended cemetery of the docks, smiling, but then he suddenly disappeared: because at the bottom of the street various policemen with their high red hair done up in a cone appeared ...

Now he stood there at our shoulders, looking at us with a shrewd and gentle smile: sideways on, every so often running off at a tangent, with his angelic clothes fluttering around him.

He followed us while, having left the rickshaw, we went through some shops towards the sea embankment. He observed us while we were making an arrangement with a boatman, and when we were about to get into the boat he was there again, looking at me with the whites of his eyes and of his teeth – in a smile of sugar. I told him to jump in: Josef said okay, and little by little the boatman began to row along the stretch of sea beyond which, in the distance, Cochin was spread out in all its length, with those gentle Dutch roofs.

We went towards the open sea: on the left the extreme point of Cochin, on the right, beyond the other stretch of sea, Enarkulam: behind, on the tip of the island in the middle of the port, the *Malabar*, alone amidst the cries of the crows: and opposite, tongues of earth heavy with palm trees – the Terrestrial Paradise.

As the boat sailed I hit up a little friendship with Revi: but, poor child, there was almost nothing to find out about him: he was from Trivandrum, another port of the Kerala and about a hundred kilometres further South. His mother, Appawali, was dead. His father, Appukutti, no longer knew anything of him. He lived like that, day-to-day, on the docks of Cochin.

I wanted to reach the nearest of the islands massed opposite the port with their paradisical palm groves: and to walk on them a little, alone, to lose myself for some time.

The first island, the one exactly opposite the *Malabar*, had a rocky bank with yellow grass extending immediately behind, an ideal place for cobras, with some tufts here and there speckled with plants. The other islands were too far for the little boat. I got off there, telling Josef and the other to wait for me. Revi, on the other hand, who was as free as a boy or a woman, did not obey me and followed me, certain that it would be enough to smile at me to convince me to excuse him. When he smiled he fixed his eyes on mine and it seemed as if he injected all his abundant gentleness into me.

I went on to make my tour round an island which was totally arid and deserted: with him behind me. At a certain point, in fact, he dared to take me by the hand. And, although he had said that he didn't know English, he began to chatter a little: otherwise we mainly communicated with gestures, with looks. He had sad little tales to tell me. And when at the end, returning to the place where we had left the boat (which was not there: it had moved away from the rocky coast), I made the gesture of giving him some rupees, he didn't want to take them. I didn't understand why and I insisted: for me it was really nothing, he could take those few rupees easily. And he continued to say no, with that happy smile. Laboriously I managed to understand the reason why: it was useless to give him those coins because the big boys would have taken them from him. "They are not good men!", he said. I told him to hide them. But where? In his rolled-up shirt. It was a pretty poor hiding-place. But it was something. Better to try. However Josef and the other man arrived, black under their white turbans and slowly they began to sail towards the *Malabar* far away amongst the cries of the ravens.

Having landed near to the hotel Revi left me at once, running away; but there was no longer a smile in the last glance he gave me; there was that naked scorched colour which gives one a sense of sudden grief: he flew away far into the funereal depths of the dock, his long white rags billowing dramatically behind him.

That evening at supper in the hotel I tormented Moravia and Elsa with my scruples: we were getting towards the end of our voyage in India, and were practically drained by the pressure of its suffering and by pity. Every time one leaves someone in India one has the impression that one is leaving a dying person who is about to drown in the midst of the flotsam of a shipwreck. One cannot resist this situation for long: in any case the whole Indian road behind me was strewn with wrecks who didn't even extend their hands in request. Revi made me pity him more than the others: because he was the only joyful one, with a Christian joyfulness. A pity which in that moment, under the lugubriously glittering lights of the *Malabar Hotel*, seemed to me unbearable.

And then even later, in the well-cut meadow in front of the hotel, by the sea, with the ravens screaming round about and in the distance the line of those tongues of earth beyond the port . . .

I decided that I had to try something: it was absurd but I couldn't do anything else. Moravia, with his well-tried shrewdness and lack of any sentimentalism, (a lack which he owed to his Roman Catholic background), advised me strongly to follow the counsels of my conscience: Elsa however, who was both an aggressive and a gentle person, wanted to join in with me, for she was attracted by the absurd. I remembered that the day before, while wandering through Cochin, we had stopped in front of a Catholic Church and had made the acquaintance of the priest of that church, a merry Indian, dark as a negro . . . I thought perhaps also at Cochin, as in Italy, there was some Catholic organisation which looked after abandoned boys. And it is true that there are millions of abandoned boys in India: but there are also millions of lepers, and just like Sister Teresa at Calcutta, here there could be someone who had as their life's ideal scooping out the sea with a little finger . . .

We called Tayaram and we filed down towards Cochin. The evening was already quite advanced and the docks were deserted. However, in Cochin all the bazaars were open, the light was glittering everywhere, and the crowd with its fantastic clothes was still wandering in groups through the little streets, beneath the battlements and the Dutch houses.

The church which we were looking for was unlit and deserted: but already there was one of those rows of little shops which stand in a tight circle, within which was a hunched proprietor like a little turkey

in a hut. There we were told that the priest had gone
to a street carnival not far away: and one of them
offered to accompany us.

The feast was being celebrated behind a high wall at
the edge of the city: through the gateway some tents
crowded with people could be picked out and, in the
background, a little stage on which, accompanied by
the usual primitive instruments, a woman was singing
who appeared like a caricature, singing over and over
the same tortured and doleful melody.

On this side of the gateway in the courtyard there
was a large crowd of passers-by and the simply curious:
it was a *Mohammedan* feast, and the faces were for the
most part Muslim, astute and modern: with the usual
chaos of children and of beggars.

Someone went to call the priest, who seemed
completely overjoyed. It was not so easy to explain the
matter to him, because the Indians understand things
rather slowly, they have complicated coordinations.
But when he had understood he said to us very simply:
"Okay, I take you to Father Wilbert!"

We travelled a long way in the car amidst the
little villas and the houses scattered below the
crooked palm trees, and we arrived in front of a little
house from which some light was still glimmering. We
got out and entered. Father Wilbert was listening to
some classical music, Bach I think, and reading papers
in a smoky little room, full of some very unvarnished
furniture, which was just like the front room of poor
people's houses. He was still young and had, like the
saints, a big beard and a lot of hair: only instead of
being black, his hair was red: a Flemish redness. He
was in fact Dutch. As he got up, I saw that he was at
least double our height. We began to negotiate: and
Elsa, who speaks English better than I, began to

explain to him. It was very simple: Father Wilbert was Dutch and not Indian: and we also understood each other by making word games. We could go to get Revi straight away: without a doubt he would put him up in his *St. Francis Boys Home*. But I asked myself (and I asked him) whether there would be some religious objective . . . No, certainly not: no work of conversion: only the example. The smiling eyes in the middle of Father Wilbert's red face convinced me. Oh, he said that by no means all who went to him remained there; many ran away, returned to the streets: but every so often they put in an appearance later on . . . He spoke of his boys like a strange phenomenon, a little mad, with a resigned smile on his big reddish features.

With Tayaram, who was as gentle as a young girl nodding in agreement who understood nothing, we returned quickly down along the docks and the shops at the bottom of the deserted port, where the lights of the *Malabar* glittered in their abandon.

It wasn't difficult to find Revi: there he was, amongst his group of ragged and ruffian friends, fresh, with his penetrating and radiant smile, as if hunger, sleep, illness, corruption, horror did not exist or didn't make any impression on him. He came along amidst his billowing rags, blown up by the wind against his body like those of the little Tobias, and he listened to me.

I said to him that I was taking him to the house of my European friend, my true friend, who would give him something to eat and a place to sleep; and who would also teach him a job; or would simply instruct him; so that he would be able to write to me in Italy and to read my letters. Then, if he was good, I would send him some little presents from Italy.

But there was no need to discuss so much with him:

it would have been enough if I said to him "Let's go": and he would have run, as indeed he did, to get into the large Ford next to Tarayam, faithful and happy, looking back every so often beyond the head rest, with those eyes of his which projected a ready, white, gentle smile like a taste of honey.

Like this we returned to Father Wilbert, and we presented the boy to him. He bent down to the earth, as tall as he was, and putting his large red beard at the height of Revi's Moorish face, began a discussion with him in very intimate Tamil. Revi replied quietly, lighting up every now and then, timid and enthusiastic. And Father Wilbert: – *papaparapaparapa* like a used magnetic tape made to run to its end, nodding his head modestly, as is the gentle custom of the Hindus.

"Well," he said at the end, promoting Revi by this rapid exam. Revi could stay. It was all done. Every now and then I would send a little money from Italy. There was nothing to do but to go. Yes, to go. I gave a last look, a last salute to Revi, upright amongst the furniture and the official papers of the Father. I grasped the enormous hand of Father Wilbert who, smiling, accompanied us to the door, as tall as a mercenary.

But when we were half way along the street, on the bridge which joins Cochin to the island in the middle of the port, Elsa noticed that she had left her precious book in the front room of the Father: We just *had* to return for that.

It was already totally dark within the little house. We rang hesitantly and noticed some dogs, those poor terrorized Indian dogs, then a light was lit and then Father Wilbert reappeared, smiling. However, as Elsa took her book from the big hands of the Father, I timidly asked if, since we had returned, we could just

47

have a little look at his house: he raised his arms to the heavens, happy, and quickly showed us the way.

We left the little front room, where he had begun again with the music of Bach, and went out. In front of us we found a little one-storey construction, behind the central body of the house, which led us into a little courtyard towards the shadowy palm tree. That was all. We approached and, under the loggia of wood which surrounded this (apparently) little shop, we saw many stretched-out bodies. Father Wilbert gave us a discreet sign to be quiet, placing his large finger on his nose, which was rusty brown above a large red beard which shone white in the moonlight, and smiled gently. When we were above that mass of stretched-out bodies he could not suppress a really loud laugh, like a guffaw: he was ashamed, a little for the poverty of his house, a little for them, his boys, stretched out there to sleep like so many tiny animals, their stomachs in the air, their few poor colonial clothes so black, and they so defenceless and clownish in their dreams.

He guided us through those scarcely adolescent little bodies which were sleeping in disorder, evidently seized by sleep in the last position in which they found themselves, whether taking the air towards dusk, chattering or playing: they seemed cut down, except for the fact of their gentle, intense breathing. Father Wilbert whispered to us that they were used to sleep like that, that they wouldn't have been able to get used to a bed: and that he wanted to leave them their habits, even that of being vagabonds if they wanted to be, even that of smoking: every improvised change would have been dangerous for his relationship with them . . . He spoke very quietly, and every now and then smiled to himself, raising his shoulders.

48

There was an angelic goodness in those eyes. He added in a whisper that within a few days he hoped to begin the construction of the second storey of the house. While he was speaking we entered the large bare, dark room.

There also was a massacre of innocents, seized by powerful dreams.

Revi was in a little corner near to the door, perhaps in a place reserved for guests, because he wasn't stretched out on the bare earth but on a kind of white material. As soon as we entered he heard us and got up. At once he lit the lamp of his smile but it was a little exhausted, spent. When we passed in front of him in order to go out on the other side he looked at me fixedly, as if terrified. I said something to him, whispering: that if he was good I would send him some presents from Italy, that we would write, that Father Wilbert was a good man. But he placed a little hand on my arm, and still looking at me with that face which no longer seemed that of a boy but rather of an adolescent, he asked me: "Will you return from Italy?" "But yes" I murmured, "I will return, I will return . . ." I no longer managed to look him in the face. There was nothing, simply nothing to do, if not to hope in Father Wilbert. Father Wilbert was there, tall in his cassock against the palm trees, which were crooked and inanimate, and he was smiling into his beard, beneath the moon, a moon lost in the heavens like in a night of pestilence.

IV

Meeting on the edge of Gwalior. The 'story' of the evening with Muti Lal. India is basically a little country . . . Impressions of the Indian middle class. The ideal Indian as regards physical beauty. Examples of the bourgeois: Rotary Club at Aurangabad, a cinemato-graphic cocktail party at Calcutta, a picnic at Tekkadi. The song of the little Indians.

It seemed like the face of San Sebastian: inclined a little towards one shoulder, the lips swollen and almost white, the eyes as if glazed with a frozen lament, and an upper lid drawn back and red. He was walking along the edge of a shady street on the periphery of Gwalior and, having noticed that I observed him for a moment, he now followed us with a sad smile.

He was covered with the usual white rags: while around him, along that street on the periphery (if periphery and centre have any meaning for Indian cities), the usual lugubrious misery, the usual shops little more than boxes, the usual little houses in ruins, the usual stores worn down by the breath of the monsoons, the usual high stench which smothers breathing. That smell of poor food and of corpses which in India is like a continuous powerful air current that gives one a kind of fever. And that odour which, little by little, becomes an almost living physical entity, seems to interrupt the normal course of life in the body of the Indians. Its breath, attacking those little bodies covered in their light and filthy linen, seems to corrode them, forcing itself to sprout, to reach a human embodiment.

In that potent odour Muti Lal followed us humbly and anxiously. Every Indian is a beggar: even he who does not do it for a profession, if the occasion presents itself will not flinch from trying to extend his hand.

51

Our hotel rose up at the bottom of an overgreen lawn, dusty, wearing the sinister solemnity of a cure resort.

Moravia, having finished his little healthy walk which he had allowed himself in the midst of that 'sea of rags', without any hesitation reached the hotel, the desperate prospect ahead of that enormous room furnished with desolate furniture, with the grey mosquito net and the dead roaches in the bath.

However I stopped at the entrance, on that peripheral road which had the aspect of a European street. I looked at Muti Lal, who was still smiling sadly, and exchanged a word with him. We introduced ourselves and he immediately told me everything about himself, as children do throughout the world. He came from Patyali in the province of Eata, where he had a family. He was working at Gwalior in a shop as a salesman. He was sleeping with some companions on the pavement. He was a Brahmin, as the associations of his name had already informed me. His skin was clear, almost white: and his features, a little unclear and delicate, were those of a bourgeois European boy. Indeed he knew how to read and write, and in fact he must also have attended a 'high school': he lit up completely when he knew that I was a journalist, he wanted to know the name of the newspaper where I wrote my articles on India: and he asked me anxiously if I would also write the 'story' of our evening. He was therefore a bourgeois.

It may have become clear that India has nothing mysterious about it, as the legends say. Basically one is dealing with a little country with only four or five big cities, of which one alone, Bombay, is worthy of the name; without industries, or almost; very uniform and with simple historical stratifications and crystallisations.

In substance one is dealing with an enormous agricultural sub-proletariat, blocked for centuries in its institutions by a foreign domination which has made certain that these institutions were preserved while at the same time, through the fault of a conservation so consistent and unnatural, that they degenerated.

In reality a country like India is easy to grasp intellectually. Although certainly one can go astray there, in the middle of this crowd of four hundred million souls: but one goes astray as in a rebus, in which one can arrive at the top with patience: the particulars are difficult, but not the substance.

One of the most difficult 'particulars' in this world is the middle class. Certainly we Italians have a model which at present vaguely approximates to the Indian one, if we think of our Southern middle class: recent formation, imitation of another type of middle class, psychological imbalance with strong contradictions, ranging from a stupid and cruel pride to a sincere understanding of the people's problems, etcetera.

However in the Indian middle class there is something terribly uncertain, which gives one a sense of pity and of fear.

Obviously we are dealing with a disproportion that is almost inhuman in relation to the reality in which it exists, in which live the enormous mass of the sub-proletarian who surround it like an ocean. It is true that the Indian middle class is born into that inferno: in those unformed and hungry cities, in those villas constructed with mud and the dung of cows, amidst famine and epidemic. Because of all this, it seems traumatised by it. It is rendered speechless or at least voiceless by it. The owners of the shops, and the rare professionals always have a terrified look, almost stupefied. In comparison to the Europeans, who are still a model that seems unreachable to them, they have almost lost their tongue.

So they fix on family life, to which they give absolute priority: they are full of children whose gentility they cultivate: their own disturbed harmony is perpetuated in this tender model of children, and so the circle of gentility is closed, rather nastily and self-centredly.

Whatever the Indian middle class is I have seen it above all in Africa, in Kenya, where there are some tens of thousands of Indians (brought there by the English to construct the railroad when the Africans were still unusable), who have become the lower middle class of the place. They have become completely washed-out. Unsympathetic to the Africans, they cultivate this family gentility around the shop which gives them the ease or even a little wealth to do so: while underneath lingers the pain of not yet being Europeans.

I remember that I was hurrying through the streets of Mombasa in a car when a silhouette crossed the street, unsure, risking being knocked down and my negro driver Ngomu hit his forehead with a finger, saying, as if one was talking of a habitual and natural topic: "Indian: stupid".

And another time I was walking through some little streets in Zanzibar at night, amidst piles or rubbish, and the two young negroes who were with me, Snani and Bwanatosha, said to me, with the same tone in their voice as they looked around: "Indian: dirty".

But it is not even accurate to speak of resignation and fatalism: because in the Indian middle class there is always a kind of anxiety, a sense of waiting, even if it is buried and useless.

Muti Lal wanted to take me to the theatre. We met each other after supper, having spent some hours in the desperate room on the ground floor of the national hotel, which seemed to be specially made for the entry of cobras; and we went together through the now dark big street, deserted but for its vague and terrible scent.

We walked for a long time in between clusters of atrocious huts, little walls on fearsome meadows, and we arrived at a kind of fair: as usual, in the darkness and with the lights lit, everything appeared artificial, fantastic, worthy of *Thousand and One Nights*.

We walked amongst the illuminated tents for a good long way, between crowds in cloaks and girdles, with turbans wound round the most beautiful hair, black and wavy, in the world, and we arrived at the theatre.

There was a large tent surrounded by a file of ragged people: some acting as guardians, others loitering and enjoying the music which floated violently, with frantic beatings of the drum, out of the tent.

Muti Lal bought the tickets and we entered.

One had to go down three or four steps of mud because the theatre was a broad rectangle in fact scraped out of the yellow mud and covered over by the big tent.

Fifty or so rows of improvised seats filled it: and one saw from close by the lined faces of the Indians with their rags and their turbans. It was cold and everyone was trembling, covered with their light linen and with only a scarf around their head. A long row of spectators was also squatting along the edge of the rectangular pit, against the tent.

Some seats stood there on their own just below the stage, at least four to five metres from each other: they were the best places. Muti Lal happily guided me there, and I sat down between him and a bearded shopkeeper, who was already absorbed in the drama.

The podium in front of the stage had not been formed by digging out the mud; since it was attached to the apron of the stage, with some improvised steps on the side made of yellow mud. The instrumentalists were gathered above there: they were playing a kind of pianola, a drum, and a wind instrument which made a deafening noise, accompanying and underlining the caressing, pathetic songs of the actors with unheard-of violence.

The actors were all fat or well nourished: they were enacting, really, a drama of adventure with various *coups de théâtre*, with refindings, deposed kings, robbers and unhappy loves: but they were all as pink as piglets, with their full faces, their beautiful penguin thighs. The essence of virility was represented in the hero, by a pair of black whiskers which appeared to be false and that stood out proudly from his pink face.

It didn't take me very long to notice that they were a disguise: beneath the white and red face one saw the black hair of his neck and his chest. The heroic and erotic idea of the Indians was one of white colouring, endowed with a respectable rotundity.

In fact in all the little towns the advertisements for the cinema, depicted in a very simple and monotonous way, all represented endless processions of white protagonists with round cheeks and a little bit of a double chin.

Now, all the Indians are minute, thin, with the little bodies of children: they are wonderful until twenty years old, gracious and full of pathos afterwards. How could such a monstrous ideal of beauty ever happen? What a difference between those stocky, puppyish heroes and my poor Muti Lal, sick, pallid, who was drinking, trembling with cold, the boiling tea, which another like him had offered him in some dirty cups.

Thus I learnt to recognise a certain type of Indian bourgeois: which to be honest is still very rare. One finds him in some large hotel or in the little waiting rooms of airports. He is massive, corpulent, with hair which would have been beautiful, like that of almost all Indians, if a clever barber had not made them similar to two wings of a raven divided on the inclined skull: he has a fat wife, dressed in a splendid pink and yellow sari, the features balanced on round cheeks, and a little hair on the upper lip: as well as a daughter clothed in the European style, curiously ugly, who laughs with the voice of a crackling gramophone.

It is the middle class which, still very discreetly, hurries to occupy the place left by the deposed but still very rich Maharajas (these are totally sold out in any case: I have seen one of them with his little court at the *Ritz*, which is the best, albeit only night spot for the rich of Bombay: he seemed like a faded puppet, dressed in the European style, surrounded by European women with whom he was dancing the waltz).

In India the vigour possessed by that unpleasant institution called the Rotary Club is extraordinary. There was no hotel where we went (and the hotels of necessity had to be first class) where we did not find some people gathered for a cocktail. However they seemed to me reunions of the dead, who were embalmed with their beautiful flaring Sari across them. I remember our arrival at Aurungabad, which was the first truly Indian town which we visited after Bombay. Before going to the hotel from the airport we wanted to pass through the centre of the city, so voracious was our anxiety to look.

It was already night. Things appeared and disappeared

57

like visions, encapsulated in clusters of lights by the indescribably "eastern" atmosphere: a mussulman arch, like a relic in the middle of a sea of huts, laid out like hunched backs, with the little shops offering materials or coloured foods, and in front of them the whirling crowd of people with light blue or red bandages on their heads, absurd clothes of an epoch light years away from ours, goats, cows, rickshaws . . . Along the edge of the central street (which was like a long vivisection, with the walls of the little houses of one storey leaning entangled one against the other, each one with an illuminated and crowded little shop in front) ran the ditches of the drains which passed under the shops, which one entered over a small rounded step . . . Observe the children who were collecting the dung of cows on the street, putting it into flat wide baskets . . . Observe the groups of young Mussulmans with their books under their arms . . . Observe a latrine, two high walls a half metre above the edge of the ditch, amongst which the Indians were urinating squatting, as is their habit . . . Observe the crows, always present throughout India with their purposeless scream . . . We crossed the entire city, which like all the Indian cities is only a big formless mass around a market. We left through another mussulman archway and, across the country dotted with school buildings and barracks inherited from the English, we arrived at the hotel. This was a light construction on one storey, most elegant, two long wings with the doors of the rooms giving onto a little portico, laid out in a large garden dotted with banjam trees and bouganvillea. As we entered into the little hall painted white with some little birds fluttering there freely, we didn't notice anything at first: but after an instant our attention was attracted by a crowd occuping this hall: gentlemen dressed in white and ladies in Sari, all seated on some chairs laid out along the walls. Either they were silent or they were talking in a whisper. They were rich people, members of the Rotary Club in fact, perfectly inconceivable in the social circle which made up Aurangabad. After a few minutes they were eating at a very long table set out under the portico of one of the wings of the hotel, silent in the intense light which isolated them from the thick darkness of the country, one not without cobras, where thousands of miserable people were sleeping in their huts or on the rude earth, like a biblical dream.

And I remember also at Calcutta: this time it was not a matter of a Rotary Club meeting but of a cocktail party in honour of some actress or another, the usual fat piece with the made-up eyes: there had been a gloomy party with music and traditional dances in the dining-room at the centre of the hotel; then the guests had wandered out into the corridors and the waiting halls, with the great hangings and the huge ventilators suspended above the pink velvets and light woods of vast colonial elegance: they were all half drunk (the Indians get drunk easily: and in many states there is prohibition), lugubriously happy: but silent. They didn't know how to exchange conversation. And one understood that around their cocktail party extended Calcutta, the unconfined city where every human pain and suffering touches the extreme limit, and life is carried out like a funereal ballet.

The people in India that I have studied, whether they possess something or carry out that function one calls 'governing', know that they have no hope: scarcely freed from the inferno by means of a modern

cultural conscience they know that they will have to
stay in that inferno. The horizon of even the most
vague renaissance is not visible in this generation, nor
even in the next, and who knows in which of the
future ones. The absence of every realisable hope
makes the Indian middle class, as I said before, enclose
themselves in that little certainty they possess: the
family. They huddle there in order not to see and not
to be seen. They have a very noble civic sense: and
their ideal heroes, Gandhi and Nehru, are there to
testify to it: they possess a quality which is absolutely
rare in the modern world: tolerance. This, despite the
impossibility of acting, forces them into a state of
renunciation which reduces their mental horizon: but
such modesty is infinitely more touching than
irritating. And this is certain: it is never vulgar.
Although India may be an inferno of misery it is
wonderful to live there, because it almost totally lacks
this vulgarity. Even the vulgarity of the 'hero' with
which the Indian identifies himself (the pink puppy
with black whiskers) is in reality absolutely ingenuous
and comic, generally common to all peasant societies.
The big puppies with their black whiskers, vulgar in
the true sense of the word (be it in type contaminated
by imitation of a foreign middle class, more precisely,
by Americanism), are very rare. At Tekkadi, a place
lost in the heart of the South, I saw two types of
different middle-class people: exactly in proportion to
their numbers.

Tekkadi is a tourist place: hotels are grouped on the
boundaries of Kerala and the state of Madras, in the
middle of a forest, on the banks of a large artificial
lake. One goes there because they say there are some
wild animals: indeed it is true that a tour by boat on
the lake at dawn, the hour in which the animals go to

drink is included in the tourist programme. In reality we didn't see a single thing, and I had to seek the innocent pleasure of seeing wild animals roaming freely in Africa.

The day on which we arrived in Tekkadi was the day of the tenth anniversary of Indian independence. Throughout all the villages we crossed one felt this simple atmosphere of a noble national festival because, as I was saying, India is an extremely simple and provincial country. There were flags and bunting on the poor huts amidst the palm groves, columns of school children through the streets, and gatherings of people seated formally in the middle of dusty village squares.

Many groups had made an excursion to Tekkadi for the festival: but let's be clear, there was much simplicity and poverty. However the atmosphere was that of certain European tourist spots on a Sunday.

Evening was descending: the lake in front was fearsome in its primordial silence, inimical to man. But around us we heard voices, the laughter of groups.

Before supper Moravia and I went on a little walk along the road by the hotel which, with its rather Swiss aspect, rose up on a long promontory of the sad lake.

While we were walking a 1100, a black one (yes, a 1100, a Fiat, which is a very common car in India) came towards us, full of four or five rather fat young men, pink, with black whiskers: it pretended to come across our path, with an insolent hooting of the horn: nothing else. But this was the only pathetic, aggressive and vulgar act of our whole Indian stay: something worthy of Milan or Palermo. Heaven preserve that this is not the way of evolution of the scarcely-formed Indian middle class. Certainly objectively there is a danger. The weak have a strong tendency to become violent, the fragile to become ferocious: it would be terrible if a population of four hundred million inhabitants, which at the moment carries such weight on the historical and political stage of the world, became westernised in this mechanical and degrading way. There is everything to wish for this people apart from the middle class experience, which would end up being of the Balkan, Spanish or Bourbon type. However those fat fellows with their whiskers were only four; nothing in comparison with the whole school with its teachers who we met a little while after as we were continuing our walk.

They were all dressed in white: but this time the cloth was really white and new, because it was a holiday, because it was the day of independence. The big sheet around the hips or held down as far as the ankles, or taken by the corners and tied on the stomach in such a way as to leave the leg bare, the little tunic or white blouse, the white turban bound round the black wavy hair, with its weight and curls so romantic and barbaric: all was clean and pure.

They were standing at the bottom of a grassy slope on the edge of the lake, which had already disappeared in the last blood-red colours of dusk.

We went to sit on the slope opposite them, and we began to look at each other a little timidly. What a difference to our students! These were behaving perfectly, almost silently, chattering amongst themselves or with their teachers almost in a whisper. However the happiness of the moment and of the occasion shone in their eyes, black and brilliant in their dark faces, those tender and modest features. They looked at Moravia and I, sometimes scarcely noticing us, other times giving us a full smile. But they didn't dare address us, and we were also silent, as if through fear of interrupting that current of sympathy, which although silent was so full. Also they seemed to have understood, teachers and students, that the best thing was to look and smile at us like that, in silence.

Five, ten minutes passed, a quarter of an hour. The light of dusk became ever more gloomy, and there we all were, opposite each other, looking: their clothes belonging to the ancient pagan world became ever whiter, their silent sympathy sweeter.

Then, after having exchanged some words almost in a whisper, one of them, who was nearer on the gentle slope, came forward to where we were sitting: his companions were seated around him, cross-legged on the dry grass; in his hand he held a recorder or a flute, I don't know, but a little wind instrument: almost hidden amidst the folds of his tunic. He was uncertain whether to play or not: and his companions smiled, encouraging him. Then he decided. He sat on the grass and, with his face turned towards us, began to play. It was an old Indian melody, because India is resistant to any kind of foreign musical influence: indeed I believe that the Indians may not even be physically capable of hearing music other than their own. It was a syncopated, muffled and doleful phrase, which always finished, as with every Indian air, in an almost guttural lament, a sweet, pathetic death-rattle: but a kind of noble, innocent happiness was enclosed within this sadness.

The boy played his flute and looked at us. It seemed as if, by playing to us in that way, he spoke to us, he made us a long speech, for himself and his companions.

"Look at us here", he seemed to say, "poor little Indians, with these clothes of ours which scarcely cover our small bodies, naked and dark like those of animals, lambs or little goats. We go to school, it is true, we study. You can see our teachers around us. We have our ancient religion, complicated and a little terrifying, and in addition today we celebrate with flags and little processions the festival of our independence.

"But how far there is still to go! Our villages are constructed with mud and with the dung of cows, our cities are only markets without form, dust-ridden and impoverished. Illnesses of every kind threaten us, smallpox and plague are at home here, like snakes. And so many younger brothers are born for whom we cannot find a handful of rice to divide amongst them. What will happen to us? What can we do? However in this tragedy there remains in our souls something which, if it is not happiness, is almost happiness: it is tenderness, humility towards the world, it is love ... with this smile of sweetness, you, lucky foreigner, when you have returned to your homeland you will remember us, poor little Indians ..."

He continued to play and to talk like this, for a long time, in the anguished silence of the lake.

V

Difficulties with the historicist "analysis" in its attempt to analyse the traditional Indian castes. What constitutes the sense of identity for the Hindu: the degenerate fixation. Examples of such fixation (which has nothing of miserable European conformism): the customs, the eating ritual, etcetera. The "codified" death of an old woman dressed in green at Ajanta. Types of Indian intellectuals: poets, critics, journalists . . . Pathetic irritations with Nehru.

Nehru has declared openly in front of all his four hundred million citizens that he is not a believer, that religion is certainly a fine thing but in fact it doesn't interest him.

This extraordinary liberty of thought, this pure lack of hypocrisy is one of the most important facts of the time in which we live.

Make no mistake: I would say the same thing if a president of the Chamber, a religious man, said in front of his four hundred million non-believing subjects that he is a believer. For now I cite the case, a real and not hypothetical one, of Nehru. We should make a strong note of this in our conscience: a conscience which in these last years, precisely with the arrival on the scene of history of the under-developed nations, from India to Indonesia to Africa, is beginning to be discontented with being merely European and is trying to make itself world-wide. Seen in this way national traditions shrink to a modest size, become fussy and irrelevant. Nehru was born at Allahbad, a city in the plain of the Ganges, of a middle class family: but his upbringing is English. And he has absorbed the most typical quality of English culture: empiricism. Now Nehru is neither English nor Indian: he is a man of the world, who with an Indian gentility and English practicality is occupied with the problems of one of the great countries of the world.

There is therefore a notable distance between Nehru

and India: a distance which in certain moments is an abyss. India is in fact still immersed in its national traditions, which in turn are splintered into a thousand different national traditions, as many as the states which make up the Indian federation. It is true that geographically, racially, architecturally, there is a uniformity in India which concedes nothing to that of France or Holland: a uniformity which in fact approaches obsession and monotony. But the sense of diversity is secret and interior: it is due to another type of tradition from that which our historicism is used to considering: a historicism made easy precisely by the very obvious storico-geographic, stylistic, folklore differences in Europe. In India the tradition is a *caste* tradition. And its rigidities glide over the 'internal surfaces' of the country: it is therefore very difficult for the historicist "analysis" to isolate and study them.

Besides they have been preserved in obviously complex conditions, that is to say, through the various static surroundings provided by successive foreign domination: for this reason their conservation is really a degeneration.

The Indians at the moment are an immense population of disturbed and hesitant people: like people who have lived for a long time in the dark and are suddenly brought into the light.

Their reaction is gentle, a well-controlled and humble astonishment. But that whole terrible shadow from which they have barely escaped continues to weigh threateningly on their horizon. For example: the castes have been abolished. Life now proceeds as if such an abolition were real: in reality it still is not. The Indians perhaps think of it every moment of the day, in every circumstance. But for an observer like me the matter had an ambiguous, elusive side.

Is it really true that the Untouchables no longer exist? In practice I gave my handshake to everyone whom I met and they all gave theirs without embarrassment: and yet trustworthy witnesses, both Indian and European, continued to insist that Untouchability had not in fact disappeared.

Is a modern population conceivable in which there are millions of Untouchables? And then the Indians are enormous in number and in continual growth: they are not even numberable, so to speak: indeed a civilian status does not yet exist. The only difference between one individual and another is in practise his belief and his religious rite: and it is precisely to this that individuals attach themselves with mad tenacity, specialising in a cult which serves nothing. It is pure, crazy, ritual exterior.

However, every Indian tends to "fix" himself, to recognise himself in the mechanics of a custom, in the repetition of an act. Without this mechanism and this repetition his sense of identity would receive a heavy blow: it would tend to fall apart and evaporate. For this reason at all levels the Indians seem codified. It is that which is called conformity in Europe but which here, not being middle or lower middle class but traditional, from an ancient but desperate tradition, has nothing impoverished and shabby in it: the smallness to which it reduces man has something grandiose about it.

Everything in India, if you look closely, tends to be classified, that is to say, to become fixed in decline.

Of this one has infinite, if nonetheless confused examples. In the houses and hotels the duties of the servants have pathological divisions and prerogatives: a Brahmin will not be able to do that which a Sikh does, and a Sikh will never lend himself to that which an Untouchable does. To enter into a hotel signifies an entrance into the heart of a series of mad specialisations. Other mad specialisations occur during the meals: And the wives of diplomats know it well, whenever they must organise a dinner to which are invited Hindu, Muslims, Brahmins etc: there must be a hundred types of food, because eating is a ritual and the ritual cannot be betrayed.

At the lowest level, in a popular restaurant it is truly a spectacle to be present when people are eating. The Hindus, according to their ritual, must eat with the hands, in fact with one hand, I don't remember whether the left or the right: they can be spotted however as the crowds of one-handed people who scoop up the rice, dip it in the liquid curry and bear it to their mouth as in a silent wager.

Sometimes the codification has sublime aspects, as I happened to observe while passing through the village of Ajanta.

It was during the first days that I was in India: from Bombay we had gone by plane to Aurangabad and from Aurangabad in a car to the temples of Ellora and in fact to the caves of Ajanta. The heat was ferocious: summer (which in winter one always forgets) was in its full glory, the sky scorched by so much sun. Exhausted by the visit to the caves, stretched on a rocky bank along a funny little stream for tigers and leopards, we had stopped at the village for a moment. Moravia remained in the car in a shaded corner amidst the undescribable huts lined up in the dust: I was not able to resist a little walk.

Little things struck me again with an unexpected violence: pregnant with meaning and, so to speak, with expressive power. The colours of the womens' peplos, there were desperately glaring, without any delicacy, greens which were maroons, maroons which were violets; the gold of the little wash-tubs for water, small and precious like jewel caskets; the swarms of people dressed in billowing wraps; the smiles on black faces under white turbans: all was glittering to the cornea, impressing it with an almost wounding force.

I walked through the street powdered with dust, pressed in between the rows of little houses signalled by steps above the drainage ditches, and small like stables, of painted wood; for the most part they were the usual little shops with the salesmen squatting inside; bananas and pineapples were displayed on the ground, with groups of boys and youngsters around, under the contorted shadow of some banjan tree with its roots finishing among the branches; and lines of women were walking amidst the dirt leading children with painted eyes. Then the street turned to the right towards a tiny mediaeval arch of stone, and at its feet were crouched some little bandits with moustaches on their upper lip, as if removed from some altar-piece.

There the houses were really chicken huts: in one of them, small as a puppet stage and grey with filth, there were two, three nude children. They were looking at me fixedly, every so often shouting at me a word like "Natan, Natan!" behind my back.

On the other side of the little street, all dust and sewage mud, there was another tiny house: of stone this one, with a high step. Above this step an old woman was stretched out just by the threshold. She seemed fixed to the stone. As if in a nightmare, it seemed as if she wanted to rise and could not. She was evidently in agony. As thin as a child, stamped with knots of poor contracted nerves, she lay there supine, with her neck on the stone, moving her head from right to left.

Her dress was green, of a flaming green, and it was completely open in front: her shrivelled bosom was uncovered. Some children who had followed me were now also looking at her with me: and also in their gaze there was slight dismay, but as if resigned and of little matter.

I stepped further towards her: towards the step and towards that little dry sewer which was running beneath. The lurid green of the cloth, the dark and shrunken skin . . . But from close up I noticed that the movements of the mouth, which seemed pure motions of anguish, of intense suffering, were in fact words, sounds. The dying woman was singing. It wasn't really an articulate song but a dirge, a *cantilena*. Besides, every Indian song is like that. Grief, fear, spasm, torture has found that form in which to be crystallised: they escape their intolerable particularity by becoming systematised, almost ordered, in that poor mechanism of words and melody.

It was little more than a murmur which issued from that naked and contracted chest, from those poor limbs which had reached the end of their physical life, dressed in green girlish clothing: and yet it was enough to transform the intolerability of death into one of the many desperate but tolerable acts of life.

In this case, I repeat, the codification (or ritualisation which gives shelter to the psychological misery of the Hindu) had something sublime in it. In other cases one has exactly the opposite process. One arrives, that is to say, at the sordid, the unclean. Suffice it to quote as example the atrocious decline which hygienic measures have suffered.

I assume that, originally, both the untouchability and the ablutions would have had a hygienic significance, even if one is dealing with an assumption

71

which seems banal. Now one only needs to go by boat on the Ganges, perhaps comfortably seated on the upper deck, in order to see what these ablutions have become. In the water of the Ganges are immersed corpses before being burned: in the water of the Ganges are thrown, not burnt but fixed between two slabs of stone, the holy ones, those with smallpox and the lepers: in the water of the Ganges gather and float all the rubbish and the filth of a city which is practically a mortuary, because the people come there to die. And yet in this very water one sees hundreds of people carefully washing themselves, diving in happily, staying there immersed as far as their stomachs, rinsing themselves a thousand times, washing their mouth and their teeth: all accompanied by mechanical, neurotic gestures, yet made with great naturalness, almost with transcendence, which is usual in the Indian rites.

I said at the beginning that for these reasons the difference between the India of caste and its leader educated at Cambridge is sometimes really an abyss. And yet, and yet ... even in the legal exactitude of Nehru, in his hair-splitting and almost obsessive defence of the parliamentary system, there is something of that paralysing codification which is typical of all the Indians. One feels that the British parliamentary grammar has been assimilated by someone who had other grammatical habits. Indeed, whoever is brought up in his own grammar is capable, if necessary, of transgressions, of exceptions and even scandalous innovations, which are however the very life of his institutional grammar: whereas whoever is unused to such a grammar will never dare to accept transgressions or attempt innovations. His obedience to the norm will be pedantic, perhaps in a sublime way, as it seems to me in Nehru. It is for this reason that, on my visit to India I felt towards its leader, who is adorable in other ways, a lot of emotional anger . . .

The same respect for the normative and known is shown by the Indian newspapers: but often in a ridiculous way: the daily papers of Bombay and Calcutta, that is to say of two infernos, seem to be those of Zurich or Bellinzona. Small characters, aristocratic lay-out, perfect language, gracious and not without some humour.

In such a case codification has the well-known characteristics of conformism: in fact we are no longer at a popular level, but at a middle class and intellectual one.

In India about 85 per cent of the people are illiterate (who for the most part however are highly cultivated in their own circle): one might guess therefore the small number of intellectuals who, for good or ill, operate and reason and behave at the level of Nehru: and who may be in a position to collaborate with him.

I had occasion to meet many of these Indian intellectuals. Indeed I went to India precisely on the pretext of an invitation to the commemoration of the poet Tagore, who is considered the greatest modern Indian poet, but who is really little more than a dialect poet: a Barbarini or a Pascarella to be frank,[3] with much spiritualism in him, as well as our everyday qualunquismo.[4]

As soon as we arrived at Bombay, Moravia and I assiduously participated in the work of this congress. It took place outside, on the lawn of a theatre along the main street of the city. A huge tent had been erected on the summer lawn, and the luxurious folds of cloth were doing nothing else but float in the tepid breezes, in the pungently wafting scent of India. Under the awning swarmed a crowd of dignitaries, of scribes, of servants, of princes: or at least people dressed as dignitaries, scribes, servants and princes. Even their scarves, white or yellow or orange, and the coloured Sari of the women, were fluttering in that ineffable wind, the residue of other historical epochs.

At the end of the tent a little platform was erected where in the warmth of the gentle summer, one which both infects and exhausts, the speakers alternated in front of powerfully effective microphones. They were poets, critics, journalists, come from all the states of India to give their own testimony of the celebrated poet: one had the small, almost mongoloid features of the North: another the fine face of the Centre, brown and framed by superb wavy hair: another with a heavy and big-boned mountain body like an old peasant: another with the little agile body of the Indians who swarm the bazaar. And all with the most different costumes: from that very elegant type which Nehru used to wear, with narrow trousers and a dark belt drawn around the hips, to the orange tunic of the Buddhists, the cloth draped on the shoulder like the ancient Greeks, the famous sheet made to pass between the legs with the calves uncovered; and finally to dress which was rather awkwardly European. But a profound conformism united and distinguished everyone which made one almost pity them. Nobody considered for a moment giving a true and personal critical testimony, with whatever element of surprise, illegality or scandal this might imply: they merely dedicated themselves to giving an affectionate tribute, to revealing a rhetorical thought written with "all one's soul". Amidst the indifference of the general public who received everything with the greatest apathy: given that it had a similar state of the soul to that of the speakers, of immobility instead of action, imprinted with a similar weariness: as if by a traumatic bewilderment, or by malnutrition.

I got to know other intellectuals from closer at hand. At a cold buffet given by the Italian ambassador in Delhi, Giusti del Giardino, apart from various other ambassadors and elegant ladies I met some typical Indian intellectuals: Mulaokar, director of the *Hindustan Times*, Prem Mhatia, director of the *Times of India*, Asoka Mehta, leader of the socialist party "Praja" who, to be frank, remained extremely vague and distracted in the face of my insistent and important questions; Durga Das, a political journalist who, on the contrary, was rather impressed (but perhaps through courtesy) by my discourteous observations on the Indian newspapers; and finally two writers, the famous Panikkar,[5] author of a book on the relationships between the East and Europe, also published in Italy, and the little Chandhuri,[6] a humorous writer (author of a book entitled, ironically, *Passage to England*) wearing the familiar look of a Veneto station master and collector of woodcut drawings, who was inanely trying to escape from conformism by way of the paradox and ineffectual anarchy.

The only intellectual I met in India who was gifted with a recognisable vitality was a young man of twenty three years, Don Moraes,[7] son of a director of a big newspaper who was in his own right a man to be much respected: but one who was depressed by the Indian tragedy which he had experienced through and through. The son, however, young, fresh from Cambridge, has an air about him which is rather existentialist, rather beat, perhaps a little bit unpleasant: but in him one registers a disquiet and an impatience in his way of seeking a relationship with his country, which absolutely distinguishes his approach from the intellectuals of the preceding generation.

I had seen his book *Going Away* on the table of the Italian consul Lavison (in his splendid bungalow on Malabar Hill) and at first sight, even with my poor knowledge of English, it seemed to me interesting. Moravia then read it and found it good. The only modern and energetic thing which had come into our hands.

The habit of classifying and making hierarchic (which in the end indicates within the intellectuals, apart from rational weakness, the typical sweetness and humility of the Indians) derives from that terrible mental archetype which alone informs every way of thinking and acting in India: the principle of caste. Because of it the intellectual retains the classifying and ordering principle: one which fixes things and ideas in a kind of immobile picture which does not change without anxieties and anguish. The same anxiety and anguish which visibly appear on the faces of waiters if one asks them something which is different from the menu or their habits.

That is not to say however that even in the intellectuals (poor lost souls in that enormous Buchenwald which is India) the caste spirit in its pure form, its essential form cannot be found. Some worthy people told me of a personage being watched by the governing elite, who as soon as he returned from England, where he had long contacts with political and cultural personalities (and where, in addition, he had studied at Oxford or Cambridge), piously drank the urine of a cow in order to purify himself from such contacts.

I am not losing the thread with these colourful stories, but I would like to say that it would be nice, for love of India, a love from which no visitor can draw away, if Nehru took notice that the state of India *is* a "state of emergency": and that for this reason some transgressions might be allowed from the rigid parliamentary grammar, not only allowed but thought necessary. Without a government of emergency it is difficult to be able to drag the Indians away from their 'caste death', i.e. to make a single step forward towards India. The youngsters are ready for this: if the twenty-year old intellectual Don Moraes already presents some different characteristics from the preceding generation, there are still thousands, indeed hundreds of thousands of "pariah" youngsters who, in order to take the money they have earned, no longer extend their hands to a plate so as not to be touched, genuflecting in a ritual pose as their fathers still do.

The caste tradition is a cancer extended and rooted in the whole social fabric of India. Nehru has the prestige to attempt to eradicate it by force: at least as long as he ignores the fact of being a Brahmin too.

VI

*Goodbye Delhi: a very long trip on a Dodge
with a Sikh, rushing through the whole plain
of the Ganges. The things which can be seen
there. The St. Peter's of India. Prisoners of
Abdullah and Bupati. Suspicious relations of
Moravia with the dakoyt and the kitchen.
Sublime moments at Khajuraho and a
Leopardian evening at Chattarpur. Ah, the
Clark's Hotel! Around the funeral pyres at
Benares: the only sweet and serene hour.*

Goodbye Delhi. With a pleasant feeling of happiness in the body, happiness for the long voyage which awaits us, we leave in the chill of dawn, with the sun pale on the gardens, the bungalows, the great streets of the ministry-city, of the embassy-city, of the cocktail-city. (Poor city too, in which the Western aspects are irremediably sunk in the melancholy of too large spaces, spaces within which there is always a derelict banjan with its roots in the air, a dog, a poor person: testifying to the invincibility of poverty).

Goodbye Delhi. A wide plain begins, discoloured, like an animal's skin left to sun and rain for endless seasons. There are factories, muddy, with little chimneys on the horizon, amongst large squares of canary-coloured wheat, dazzling: every so often one has the impression of being on the Paduan plain immediately after the war, when the ruins from the air-raids were still new.

But the immediate future is full of promise. A long trip into the heart of India in a Dodge as large and stable as a bus, Moravia and I alone: adapting, happy, as curious as monkeys, with all our instruments of intelligence ready for use, voracious, enjoying ourselves but ruthless. As far as the practical guarantees are concerned, we are in an iron grip: the relentless programme, which is due to the foresight of Moravia and the solicitude of his relative Cimino, a diplomat at Delhi, includes stop-overs, meals, dinners and hotels in an uninterrupted series. There is only one thing missing: Khajuraho (which is also the most anticipated stop); there are no rooms to be let. It will be necessary to ask the 'collector' at Chattarpur: and watch out, for who knows what will happen. But anyway we will arrange it . . . For now we enjoy this delicious, this frightening dash across India.

And just look . . . a closed level-crossing, on a high escarpment with a single platform . . . two or three hovels around it worn down by the sun and the monsoons . . . in the distance lime-kiln works, barracks or factories, spread out on the dusty terrain. The car stops at the top of a little ramp on the slope to wait, on the surface of the street are all sharp stones. As if nursed by the earth a snake-charmer jumps out, earth-coloured too, and from an earth-coloured basket he draws forth his cobra. He crouches with his earth-coloured servant beside him and whistles, *pirupiru pirupiru*, on his instrument. The horrible snake swells its cheeks and at once a mythical halo forms around its idiotic nose: with that nose it launches itself obstinately in an attempt to bite the hand of the player, who at each little bite of his subordinate, wrings his hand, poor man, in a silent "Ah, ah".

Then some beggars arrive with their children as little as slugs (with two-toned eyes, painted a deep black-violet, which makes little idols of them), incorrigible beggars: the living archetypes of our gypsies. And they surround us in a circle of naked limbs, of blackmail, of threat, of contagion, of rapacity, of anguish.

While around about scream the crows.

☐   ☐   ☐

The screams of the crows follow us, more or less
continuous and disordered, through the whole of India.
It is a significant iteration: it seems that they are
saying: we are always here, because India is always
like this. Apart from the madness which dominates
that brief squawk, insolent, idiotic, and shameless: the
air of someone who respects nothing, sacrilegious
without reason. And with that persistent pouring into
the ear we watch the landscape change, like an
unconfined back emerging from the dust. But a real
change never happens. In reality it remains the same
for hundreds of kilometres, from Bombay to Calcutta.

The road, narrow, surrounded by two slopes of rusty
earth and by an interminable, stupendous gallery of
banjan and other plants similar to our chestnuts,
unwinds across two landscapes which are always the
same: either uncultivated spaces, scorched, with some
thickets of deciduous wood, or spaces of haphazardly
cultivated earth, with canary-coloured spots of
dazzling millet.

Endless lines of peasant wagons continually hinder
the traffic. They are primitive wagons, those invented
by man two or three thousand years ago: a big box on
two full wheels and, in front, the buffalo which
patiently drags the old weight of human limbs, dark
and covered in their white cloth, or some heaps of
bamboo.

Our driver, who is a Sikh, curses them continually,
these poor peasants on their wagons: and it is
worthwhile to see how they regard him: a distant
smile in their eyes with the heavy eyebrows, a slight
lowering of the head under the black curve of
beautiful hair: nothing else. And he, the old Sikh,
ready to spit out his oaths. I must say that I felt an
immediate dislike for our driver and the Sikhs in

general: those Indians with long hair, a beard and a turban. Their military tradition irritates me, their proverbial loyalty, their air of "Glorious soldiers", their fame as good servants.

For this reason I would give as good as I get to our Sikh, in place of those humble peasants who, with Gandhian patience, didn't even listen to him.

What else is there on the road? The villages. At a certain point amidst the wonderful trees and the squalid expanse of huts appears a pond of dry mud in the middle of white banks. There are some women or children around it, washing themselves or their own clothes. Sometimes there is no one. Immediately afterwards the village appears: a heap of little walls which are also white, made with mud or the dung of cows, with the roofs of straw above. In the middle, dusty spaces full of goats, cows and buffalo. Suddenly the swarming begins, like so many coloured ants. It is the bazaar, the central street of the village: a whole row of shops held up by wooden feet, with merchants and salesmen crouching inside while in front the whirlwind of old people, children, women, continues with their coloured clothes and their sweet smiles amidst the filthy hump backs of the wandering cows.

☐　　☐　　☐

We arrive at Agra. Casual outskirts, unlike anywhere else, with colonial public buildings of only one storey, white and abandoned in the midst of the leprosy of the hovels. Herds of women covered in green Sari, violet Sari, red Sari, and all braceleted at the wrists and ankles, who work like chisels in the middle of the lugubrious dusty squares. Little bridges on the streams of the Genesi, with its beds dry and laid out with clothes of every colour, shining in the sultry winter sun, on the stones, on the burnt grass. Stupefied cows, groups of schoolchildren, men on big bicycles with a sheet between their legs which flutters sadly in the wind.

At Agra there is the Taj Mahal. The St. Peter's of India. It is truly a temple, or better a Muslim tomb, not a Hindu one. But it is however the national architectural form, the emblem of Air India, the dream of English spinster ladies.

There one takes off one's shoes in the vast square in front: and with the hardly repressed anger which is caused by removing one's shoes for the hundredth time, one enters amongst groups of tourists dressed like beggars – and beggars as quiet as tourists: amongst rows of girls skinned down to the bone, in Sari, guided by humble teachers; amongst groups of young students (twin brothers of the Roman ones) who come here, perhaps avoiding school.

The cacophony is far away, beyond the curve of a large muddy river, scattered with buffalo and adorned with dresses of a thousand colours: here there is a certain peace.

A high step with a front of a hundred metres, all in marble: the door, with a stairway of marble; the courtyard, hanging, of marble, with a long canal for ablutions in the middle, amidst little scraps of clean meadow; at the sides, along the walls of marble, the four doors of marble and, opposite, the great building, similar to our baptistries, of marble, with a minaret of marble. All glitters white and cold against the sky which stretches out behind it on the curve of the great river.

A real ice palace. Muslim poetry, practical and unfigurative at the same time, pragmatic and anti-

realistic at the same time, is to be found in India as if
in a world which is not its own. The corpse-like
sensuality of the Indian landscape supports, like a
foreign body in its Salgarian spaces[8], monuments of the
Muslim conquerors. Closed in their abstract
functional geometry like embellished prisons.

Even *in* the Muslim Indians there is something
ambivalent: as if a foreign body had entered within
them, a life of another nature grafted onto their
nature. I would have to stay longer in India to be able
to explain myself: mine is only an irrational
impression. If the Indian loses his insecurity, his
gentleness, his fragility, his passivity, what does he
become? The Koran hardens. It gives out certainties,
cultivates the identity. For that reason I do not find
myself at ease with Indians of the Muslim religion – in
fact a very high percentage: for my sympathy has run a
course of powerful but impalpable disillusion.

Near to Agra, but about twenty miles away, there is
a dead city, constructed by Muslim conquerors and at
once abandoned due to the aridity of its surroundings.
It has remained almost intact. A broad circle of wall
gathers all around in a wide ring, the countryside and
some miserable village which has gone up in recent
times. In the centre, above the irregular humps of a
hill, the city centre is constructed, in turn surrounded
by high walls. All of red tiles, with here and there
some clusters of arabesques in marble.

I cannot hide my attraction for these dead but intact
cities, – for pure architectures. Often I dream of them.
And I feel an almost sexual transport towards them. It
was stupendous. I would never have left there. There
was the mosque, in a vast courtyard all paved with red
tiles, with the decorated basin of marble in the middle,
and a large, stupendous, ecstatic green tree: the

mosque was a single *folie*, a mad embroidery of marble yellowed through age, with consumptive veins and white spots of freshness. Around about there were little palaces which basically had the colour and the size of our most beautiful *trecento* palaces: a sumptuous and profane Romanesque. From courtyard to courtyard one passed to the palace of the king, to the palace of the women, to the palace of meetings, to the palace of the "divan" where subjects were received. All intact, open to the sun and to curiousity.

Every time that one goes to visit a monument in India one falls prisoner to the guide, and thereafter to the crowd of beggars. A peace-disturber of rupees and small change: exasperating because one never has enough money. In the "dead city" of Agra we fell prisoners of Abdullah, a little Indian adolescent of Muslim religion. Then added to him, as we passed along the courts and courtyards, the outside stairways and steps, a Hindu colleague, Bupati.

Abdullah was shameless, Bupati timid; Abdullah got tired of following us, and Bupati would never have left us: Abdullah showed a certain irony for our unhidden admiration, and Bupati the greatest respect; Abdullah always stayed behind us, and Bupati was always at our side; at the end Abdullah asked for a tip, for him and for a woman who came to offer us some perfume sticks; Bupati, however, asked for nothing and lowered his eyes, merely extending a gentle hand.

In the Dodge we got back to the centre of the great countryside and the jungle. The road runs infinitely on. Moment by moment there is a smell, a colour, a sense which is India: every fact, even if the most insignificant, has the weight of intolerable novelty.

Along the Indian streets (inherited from the English: who grow immensely in prestige after this visit to their old colony), there is truly a extraordinary number of little buses. They are vehicles of an age which it is difficult to define: extremely angular, I could almost say bony: scaringly narrow, reduced to the bone, or rather to the rusty iron. Absolutely tiny: little more roomy than wheelbarrows, with a motor which one starts with a handle in front like in the old films. All painted in vibrant colours, from sky blue to green, from rust to red: and on the front, in flowery letters for anyone who might have doubts, is written PUBLIC CARRIER.

One meets dozens of them in every corner of the street: full of sombre and gentle Indians, of mothers, of children who never cry.

We are crossing the territory of the *dakoyt* who are lawless people, bandits who attack cars, kidnap the passengers and sometimes kill them. The *dakoyt*, together with the *cuisine*, have been the principal source of laughter on our voyage: or rather more precisely, the source of laughter was Moravia's relations with the *dakyot* and with the *cuisine*. Relations made up completely of nuances: suspicions, dissatisfactions, discontents, bitter delusions, resigned anger. The mere idea of the *dakoyt* seemed to be unpleasant in the acute, careful meditations of my adorable travelling companion. He did not speak of them, but when he spoke of them one felt that he had thought much about it. In fact it is true that at Delhi in his meeting with Nehru he had, amidst other matters, brought up the question of the *dakoyt*: one never knows, it is better to have direct information, and the most trustworthy possible. Therefore, cleverly pretending with his boyish humour to have the greatest indifference and the most objective desire for information, he had sounded out the situation in his long talk with Pandit. He was completely reassured by it: and I saw his eyes shine with intimate satisfaction. It was a great relief to no longer have this unpleasant preoccupation. Just imagine therefore the terrible disillusion when point-blank our Sikh began, in that polite military tone of the master-servant, to tell us of the *dakoyt* as if they were almost tangible: and to enumerate for us one by one their fastidious habits. I saw Moravia's eyes slowly fill with an intense displeasure, like a cheated schoolboy. And it was something which seemed to me, perhaps impolitely, irresistibly funny.

No sign of the *dakoyt*. A great desert with geologically primitive rivers, from one empty bank to the other full one. And the first and only two domestic elephants of the whole of India, who were proceeding very slowly down the dusty road.

Stupendous the fort of Gwalior: a mauve colour, with the remains of sky-blue majolica along the parapets. And stupendous the vision of the city, below, white enough to hurt the eyes. A military area, clean and full of barracks.

At the hotel (a state hotel, with a big garden in front for a rare tourist tea) we receive the good news that at the hotel of Khajuraho there is definitely no room. What to do? Stay there, go directly to Benares, choose another city? There is one possibility in the "collector" at Chattarpur. But what if he cannot do anything?

□　　□　　□

The usual pond, the usual little houses of mud walls, the usual mad mixture of goats, cows and human beings . . . But then, we see a larger pond. A true and proper *tank*, and along the pond an expanse of city, with walls of tile and chalk, finally two-storey houses, a square, however much sunk in the usual chaotic Asiatic poverty . . .

In this square, swarming with vendors and above all with soldiers and gendarmes with their imaginative uniforms, the mass of hair in a cone – the hair all dressed – or in their brilliant turbans, there is the office of the "collector". We are introduced and the "collector" goes into raptures finding himself before Moravia: *Penguin Books* have made Moravia as famous in India as in Italy. For this reason the "collector" is crazy to help. Yes, he will get us a room at the "resthouse" of Chattarpur: we can go to Khajuraho without problems.

Indeed we do go to Khajuraho, and there we pass the most beautiful afternoon of our whole Indian stay. Khajuraho is almost deserted, because it consists of few houses, of a distinctive hotel, and of a modern temple. There is a certain affluence, due to the visits of tourists. However it is peaceful.

The six temples, in the middle of an immense meadow, are in their totality sublimely beautiful. We return to Chattarpur as night is falling. I hope for one of those blessed evenings in which, while Moravia goes to bed, I can go out on a tour, totally alone, like a bloodhound on the tracks of the scent of India.

However the Dodge leaves the centre of the city behind and stops opposite a very high isolated bungalow, at the top of a little craggy and dusty hill.

It is discouraging. We enter. We almost feel dizzy, because of the highness of the walls: the ceiling is twenty metres high and all riddled with symmetrical windows, four-cornered or half-moon shape, open: in the cold of the night . . . Below, it is just desolation: a large waiting hall, white, with a portrait of Gandhi on the walls: a Gandhi nude like a worm, with a very clean piece of linen around his hips and glasses on a face as cunning as a tortoise: poor, great, crazy hero! Around us ripped and threadbare carpets, groups of chairs rooted in their corners. And the rooms . . . enough to make the heart shrink: miserable little beds with mattresses of ambiguous colours, huge wardrobes, empires of beetles, and of course of cobras . . . We carry in the rigid row of suitcases, and we resign ourselves to a very long night.

It is true that I still cherish the hope of a little walk through the city. In fact we do go out. It is already dark. By the side of the big bungalow there are some hovels on the street made of beaten earth: there shine the light of a *Thousand and one nights*, but miserably, modestly, rustically.

We walk along the road that leads to the distant city, which freezes under our footsteps (we are on a height) amidst thick embroideries of sky-blue mists and almost liquid nights. But we make only a few steps along the street amidst the horrible shrubs, thinking that something horrendous might happen in our vicinity, in the shadows: a desperate growl, a fleeting death-rattle: there are jackals.

We turn back at once, our tail between our legs. The cook, in one of the shining hovels next to the bungalow, is preparing our supper: I see that Moravia's eyes shine with both doubtful resignation and renewed hope . . . In a Leopardian atmosphere some children play in front of their parents' house: one very tiny one stands within a hut and is quickly retrieved. The other, a little bigger, looks at us with full sweetness. Nearby there is also a goat with little goats still milking her, a dog, and a little parrot in cage hung on the boughs of the banjan in front of the house.

89

Moravia does not hide his close sympathy for one of
the little goats, which jumps around vivaciously,
calling his mother "Ma, Ma . . ." I would like to catch
him to stroke him, but he escapes. Then the child
pursues him and returns towards us with the little
goat in his arms. The goat is very white, the child very
black: and both have the same gentle look in their
eyes.

□   □   □

You would need to have the repetitive power of a
mediaeval psalmist in order to be able to confront the
terrible monotony of India in all its representations.
   The pond, the villages, the jungle, the cultivation of
millet, the rows of wagons with buffalos, the swamps,
the villages . . . And the cities: the market, the fetid
swarms, the bodies stunted by an impotence which is
physically both a scent and a breeze, the cows, the
lepers, the outskirts with low, long colonial
constructions, the squares full of goats and little
children . . . We stop at Allahabad: along the huge ring
roads we nurture the doomed hope of a good meal . . .
We don't even discuss it: Moravia, even now thinking
of it, becomes heavy with disillusion: two atrocious
hotels, despite the well-known funereally happy
atmosphere: in one it is impossible to enter because of
the usual meal with the corpses of the Rotary Club, in
the other one desert: from which there emerges,
miraculously, a meal visibly swarming with amoebas.
   And we arrive at Benares.
   Ah, Clark's Hotel! Here the Sikh gives us his hand
(gloved, perhaps chewed by leprosy) and goes off
content with his tip. Very luxurious, the building on
two stories, with two huge wings, with little porticoes

and terraces, stretches out amidst cascades of
bouganvillea. In the shaded corners gangs of coolies
devoured by consumption, with protruding teeth, a
fetid mask of sickness stretched over their fine and
gentle faces. And the charmer with his cobras who,
when he sees a European advance towards him, gives
us a *piru-piru-piru* with his little trumpet, and the
cobra begins to wave about saying yes. It is from him
that the Indians have learnt to say yes: and also to
dance. But if the European turns away and goes into
the dining room (to eat badly, in the English manner)
the Indian interrupts immediately: *piru-pir* . . . And the
cobra returns with his head on the edge of the basket.
With three or four servants each, they arrange us in
the delicious little rooms with their terraces and their
portico on the bouganvillea.

Because it is not late, we go out. This time our taxi-
guide is a Muslim who is round and fast. He has
coordinations similar to ours, always preceded by a
rapid "Yes sir".

□   □   □

Benares. Nothing new: the roads of the centre are great
market streets, their shops fixed under the leaning
houses with loggias of wood, and the usual hungry
crowd, dirty and half-dressed. Naturally, the cows.

But there is an atmosphere which is, shall we say,
more integral. And greater affluence, as always where
religion is the object of speculation, however poor it is.

The air is cold, like at home in the humid spring
nights. An unpleasant sense of freezing pinches at the
whole body, and gives a new sombreness to already
sombre things: everything expands and resounds with
a yet more desperate rigour.

The guide advises us not to give anyone anything, not even a little alms money. We get out of the taxi and go towards the bank of the Ganges.

We go down a street surrounded by little walls, dwellings, yards, perhaps the walls of shops, which becomes ever more narrow and dark.

It is thronged with poor half-naked beings, in the usual sordid dance of coming and going: we are surrounded by them and pressed from all sides. On a pavement glittering with who knows what terrible atmosphere rows of bodies are stretched out: it is late, and many are already asleep there on the earth, at the edge of the street. Each at his own post, where he lies down in the evening: often there are entire families wrapped in the same drapes. Someone is not sleeping but it is as if he were already in bed and was waiting to sleep while looking at the traffic. Someone still continues to beg, extending his hand. They are lepers, blind through trachoma, affected by the plague of Cochin which monstrously expands their limbs: all patient towards sickness, all obsessive towards their immediate necessities. They spasmodically extend their hand. Along the whole street there is this pitiful army, drawn up in an inextricable mass of limbs and rags. And then, since the air is cold and dark, we grope our way forwards, losing direction, without really understanding what is around us.

Then the street descends and comes out on the bank, all paved with big slabs which are also glaring fetidly: a forest of sad umbrellas and benches, filled with the faithful who are there to spend the night, and an informal mass of boats that can scarcely be seen individually; behind, the blind glitter of the Ganges.

Helped by the driver who has first negotiated a little with the boatmen, we get into a reeling boat: and this slowly detaches itself from the bottom of the steps, amidst the hazy shapes of other boats and other human beings.

While the boat slowly moves out we see the bank appear in its entirety: up above in the distance the lights shine and, in silhouette, there rises up a kind of city of Dite, but one of modest proportions, almost rustic. They are the walls of the palaces which the maharajahs and the rich construct for themselves in order to come to die on the Ganges: they are temples, hovels, protecting walls: but all are clambering and heaped up in an undescribable chaos.

Down below shine the fires, on another dock similar to the one we have just left. We now reach it, a piece of black sloping bank crowded with boats.

We arrive beneath the fires: these are the funeral pyres: three: two high ones, like the top of a ladder: and one lower, a few metres from the surface of the water.

We get off the wavering boat and, among the keels of other boats, we wander among the dust and the lime-kilns, along a wall which seems to have survived an earthquake: and so we reach the rectangle above the wall, by a pair of dirty steps where two pyres are burning.

Around the pyres we see many Indians crouched with their usual rags. Nobody weeps, nobody is sad, nobody worries to poke the fire: all appear to be waiting merely for the fire to finish, without impatience, without the least feeling of grief, or worry, or curiosity. We walk among them, they who let us pass, tranquil, gentle and indifferent, as far as the side of the pyre. One can distinguish nothing, only some wood which is well cut and bound, in the middle of which the dead person is stretched: but all is burning, and the limbs are indistinguishable from the little boughs. There is no scent, except that delicate one of the fire.

Since the air is cold Moravia and I instinctively approach the pyres, and as we approach we soon realise that we have the pleasant sensation of people who stand around a winter fire, with their fingers numbed, and who enjoy standing there, together with a group of casual friends, on whose faces, on whose clothes, the flame placidly paints its laboured agony.

And so, comforted by the warmth, we look from close up at the poor dead who burn there without upsetting anyone. Never, in any place, at any time, in any act, during our whole Indian stay, did we feel such a profound sense of communion, of tranquillity and – almost – of joy.

Notes

1. A middle-class district of Rome.
2. A Roman flea-market.
3. Tiberio Umberto Barbarini (1872-1945), a poet writing in Veronese dialect (*I due canzonieri, I sogni*).
   Cesare Pascarella (1858-1940), a poet writing in the dialect of the region of Romagna (*Villa Gloria, La scoperta dell'America*).
4. A movement of ideas related to the journal *L'uomo qualunque*, which in 1944 attempted to define the position of the "ordinary man" as opposed to the life of political institutions. *Qualunquismo* implies an indifference to politics.
5. Madhava Panikkar (1895-1963), ambassador, statesman, novelist, historian. (*India and Western domination*).
6. Nirad Chandhuri, born in 1897 (*The Autobiography of an Unknown Indian*). *A Passage to England* (1959) refers of course to E.M. Forster's famous novel.
7. Born in 1938, a poet writing in both English and his native konkani. *Going Away* is a travel book (1960).
8. Emilio Salgari (1863-1911), author of popular adventure stories set in Asia (*The Pirates of Malaysia*).